Laughing At The Dark

A Memoir Of Motherhood And Mayhem

Laughing At The Dark

A Memoir Of Motherhood And Mayhem

Deborah Dunlevy

MADISON
HOUSE
PUBLISHING

Printed in the United States of America.

First Printing, 2021

Digital Edition ISBN: 978-0-9982337-1-0

Print Edition ISBN: 978-0-9982337-0-3

Madison House Publishing
www.madisonhousepublishing.com

Quantity sales. Special discounts are available on quantity purchases by corporations, associations, and others. For details, contact the publisher at the web-address above or call 317-797-9993.

For Allison,
who insisted

—

Preface

I finished the "final" draft of this book in early March of 2020.

If you are alive while reading this, you know the significance of that month. Events around the world since March of 2020 have made it harder than ever to keep laughing. A global pandemic. Hundreds of thousands dead. Long-term quarantines. Economic disaster. Escalating racial tensions. Protests. Outrage. Political turbulence. Forest fires. This year was so inexplicably bad that I'm writing a preface to the introduction to my own memoir. Does it get any worse than that? And who knows what's coming next? As I write this, there is no clear end in sight.

When the pandemic hit, I set aside my plans for publication of this book. There were so many more pressing matters in the world and in my community. My heart and my hands were full, and my family was home all the time, working, schooling, interrupting me a thousand times a day. It wasn't a great environment for producing high level work, and honestly, from a business point of view, it didn't seem like the best year to release a memoir. Let it go, I thought. It's not the right time.

My beta readers disagreed. One by one they brought their feedback on the early drafts. This was the perfect time to read it, they said. Their kids were crawling all over them while they tried to focus. They were going to bed at night filled with dread. They needed these stories now more than ever. This year of all years.

Their input is the reason I am publishing now. This book was originally a series of short anecdotes aimed at encouraging young moms. It grew into a more complete memoir, but its goal is still the same: to let readers know that they aren't alone.

If your life is hard, if it feels impossible, it's not because you're doing something wrong. It's because life IS hard. Sometimes it's impossible. For everyone. And if we're going to survive it, we need each other. Together, we may be able to find that rare, clear-eyed joy that is miraculously possible even where joy makes no sense.

It hasn't been a great year for happiness and light. Luckily, we don't need either to laugh at the dark.

Introduction

Before I had kids, I took myself very seriously.

Like really, very seriously.

From my earliest memories, adults commented on my maturity and the grown-up way I talked. I thought that meant that other people were taking me as seriously as I took myself, and that was all the encouragement I needed to really commit to the role.

As a kid, I thought what passed for deep thoughts and talked about them with anyone who would listen. I filled notebooks with plans for my future: the house I'd live in, the community work I'd do, and, of course, my wedding. My plans were detailed and as realistic as I could make them.[1] I even developed systematic programs of self-improvement (academics, music, exercise), and I stuck to them, inching my way toward the life I intended to have.

In college, now that I was finally an adult with the independence and responsibility I'd been longing for, I discovered belatedly that what I really wanted to do was hang out with my friends and have fun. It felt like a revelation to me, but if I'm honest, when my friends and I

---

[1] Not very realistic.

were together, we mostly talked intently about all the problems in the world and how we were going to fix them. It was exciting but also familiar. Like the old days of planning a dream house or an imaginary wedding but with a side order of being a hero.

College ended. I married my best friend, Nate, the best person I knew and also the only one in the world who took himself more seriously than I did. Together, we set out to do the hardest, most important work we were capable of. We moved to South America to start church communities in urban slums. We were blessed with good mentors and well-armed with youth, strength, and a ton of sound ideals and strategies. We joined with another family and started forming a new church. We moved into a difficult neighborhood and built a new life. We had a kid, and then another, and eventually another. We flung ourselves into the real work of the world.

And life kicked our butts.

I mean we got seriously flattened.

More than once.

Which is how I learned that there are a lot of things to take seriously in this world, but I'm not one of them.

Having kids is only one of many ways to learn how small you are compared to life's problems, but for me, it was the knock-out punch. The hardest battles of my life began in the same year I became a mom. Maybe it was a coincidence. Maybe that's just when I really took on adulthood. Or maybe God also likes to laugh at the dark. All I know is that parenting in the middle of chaos was a daily lesson in humility and a personal testing ground for reconciling the awful and the hilarious.

There were huge, life-changing events. But more importantly, there were small, day-to-day humiliations.

When my first baby, Ellie, was just a couple of weeks old, we were home in the U.S. visiting churches to tell them about the work we were doing in Argentina. One Sunday morning, we arrived early to share our story with a Sunday School class, and the plan was that we would stand up again during the worship service and tell a shortened version to the whole church. Things went great in the first hour. The baby slept the entire time and woke up just as we were finishing. As I had planned, I slipped into the nursery during the break and nursed her. I knew that once she was fed, I'd be able to leave her for a few minutes while we did the more public speaking.

It was only as we were finishing up the feeding and I went to button up my shirt that I realized I had been leaking milk.[2] And I do mean in the most obvious way. Two mid-sized circles that really couldn't be mistaken for anything else. Yes, I'm serious. Yes, I felt exactly how you think I felt.

Panicked, I scanned my options. I had no handy sweater or convenient change of clothes. I had a thick coat I could wear but it would raise obvious questions. (Like, "why are you wearing your winter coat inside this toasty room?" and

---

[2] TMI? You bet. I might as well tell you now that if this story makes you uncomfortable, you should consider reading another book. It's not going to get easier from here.

"Don't you want to take that off and get comfortable?") I could refuse to get up there at all, but we had a whole spiel worked out, and doing stuff together had always been important to us.

Finally, a burst of inspiration hit me. I'd just carry the baby and use her as a shield! It would be a cultural teaching moment! In Argentina, churches don't have nurseries because people don't leave their babies behind. They hold them. They nurse them in public. They stand in the back and bounce when they get too fussy. So I'd just tell everyone that she was a part of the presentation and then I'd hold her in a strategic position until we were finished.

It worked. Sort of. Ellie wasn't crazy about being confined to the same spot for so long. Even then, the girl liked to move. At one point she started to fuss, and Nate, not knowing my predicament, offered to take her. I clung to her desperately, waving him off as I talked over the noise and told everyone (accurately) that this was how things went in real ministry. Maybe those people thought I was crazy and were humoring me or maybe they'd accept anything if the person saying it had the title of "missionary." Either way, they smiled and nodded, and we all got through it, but I was sweating bullets by the end.

After the service, while Nate shook hands with people and answered questions, the young pastor's wife came to where I sat quietly to one side and offered to hold the baby for a while. Since she was my age and fully sympathetic, I decided to tell her the truth of my situation. Her first response ("I have a sweater you could have borrowed!") quickly gave way to giggles ("I'm sorry. I know it's not funny."). And then I was laughing, too. Because the whole thing was awkward and embarrassing and stressful and completely hilarious.

And for the love of all that is holy, why didn't I just ask if I could borrow someone's sweater?

That day my new-mom body taught me a critical lesson in the value of an honest story. Life is hard and messy and humbling. By trying to cover up the mess and avoid the humiliation, I missed out on the understanding and real help I could have had. I just needed to be willing to laugh at myself and let others do the same.

In the years that followed, I learned to laugh often, usually at my own expense. And I learned to make others laugh, too. It was the only way to survive. Be honest. Be funny. Be humble. Rinse and repeat.

Full disclosure: it hasn't always gone smoothly. Sometimes honest stories that seem funny to me don't strike other people the same way. Since we moved back to the U.S. nine years ago, I've been known to unintentionally kill conversations, or at the very least, leave awkward pauses big enough to drive a bus through.

A few years back, I went to a friend's house for lunch. She had three tiny children, and when she answered the door, she opened with an apology, waving a hand at the house.

"Sorry. It's been quite a morning. The house is a mess. Please try not to notice the cobwebs in every corner."

"Oh, don't even mention it," I said. "When my kids were this age, there were so many spiders in my bathroom skylight that it rained dead ants all over the sink."

Her eyes got wide and her frozen smile clearly said, "Well. That escalated quickly."

I saw my mistake and tried to take it back. "I mean, it wasn't a big deal. I just had to sweep them up a lot, but obviously I'm never going to judge anyone's housekeeping."

She shook her head in a dazed sort of way.

So much for putting a friend at ease. Apparently dead ants raining from the ceiling aren't a source of hilarity for everyone?

But laughing when things aren't funny is how I've gotten through the most traumatic times in my life, and those are the stories I want to tell. Every day I meet people who are battling different kinds of darkness. Most of them feel totally alone. We're all muddling through hard things with the vague conviction that everyone else is finding it easier than we are. It's the craziest sort of lie, and too many of us believe it.

For me, stories are the best way to call out the truth that we aren't alone. Everyone is finding life more bewildering than they expected because living is an inherently dangerous business.

Parents especially need this reminder. In the last decade, I've received dozens of texts from new moms sure they've done something horribly wrong because they can't figure out why their baby is crying so much or why their toddler is suddenly losing his mind in the Target parking lot. I have sat across from a mom of three who just emerged from months of postpartum depression as she told me she went to bed every single night terrified that she would not wake up in her right mind. I have faced the haunted look on a dear friend's face when she confessed her fear that she would ruin her kids' lives if she left their abusive father.

I cried with all of those women. We spoke of their pain together, and we didn't flinch away. And then, eventually, we made jokes about it. Because we may have no choice but to cry, but we can still choose to laugh through our tears.

In that spirit, a few years back, when we were in the middle of one of life's truly epic crapfests, my friend and I started a running joke. Every time we were navigating the horror of the world and we heard something jarring and memorable, we'd say, "I'm going to stitch that on a pillow."

We started a list. It's gotten pretty long.

That list of future pillows is our way of vowing not to forget the ridiculous in the middle of the terrible. If pillows sound random to you, you probably didn't grow up in the eighties. My friend and I were both raised in the kind of middle-class American Christian culture where people put embroidered words in frames on their walls or on throw pillows on their couches. They always said inspiring things like "God will make a way" and "All things work together for good for those who love Him."

The ones we have planned are a bit darker. They're also funny. I contend that both things make them more inspiring than the originals. True comfort for me has always come from a generous mixture of unflinching honesty and determined good humor. That's why I made our quotes the chapter titles for this book. Because they've made me smile when I most needed to, and let's be honest, when am I ever going to embroider a pillow?

I'm still in the middle of my journey. The outcome is unknown, and there's a lot more darkness ahead. But for what it's worth, I plan to laugh all the way to the end. If you're out there trying to keep your light going, I'd love nothing more than to laugh together.

It probably won't change the world, but it might just give us the strength to keep trying.

Part One

Laughing

At Myself

1

For Such A Tiny Thing, You Sure Do Have Big Demands

It was an ordinary night in our little two-bedroom apartment in the temporary missionary residence we called home. We had been living there only a short while, having returned to Indiana from Argentina for a six-month break. That night, as often happened, friends stopped by around dinner time, and we were happy to see them. We spent the evening hanging out, sharing some food, breaking out the boxed brownies, laughing and talking. Around nine o'clock, someone suggested putting on a movie. It was one we'd recently seen and wanted to show our friends. Everyone was on board.

Except me.

I was ready for bed, maybe not right then, but no way was I going to make it to the end of a movie. Because yes, it was an ordinary night, a night like so many others, but there was one tiny exception. We had a newborn, Ellie, our very first baby: adorable, cuddly, and, without question, going to wake up every three hours all night long wanting to suck the essence of life from my already traumatized body.

"I don't think it's a good idea to stay up another two hours," I said, hating how boring and old and not-like-myself I sounded. "I'm exhausted, and Ellie will wake me up at least three times tonight."

"You can go to bed," Nate said, full of compassionate logic. "I'll show them the movie and keep the volume down so you can sleep."

I looked at him, hoping he would be able to detect the sadness and resentment and fear-of-missing-out in my soul. Surely that much emotion must be radiating from my eyes.

But empathetic as he is, Nate can't read minds, and let's face it, my eyes probably just looked tired.

"We'll be really quiet," our friends chimed in.

"Okay," I said. After all, I didn't want my identity crisis to spoil anyone's fun.

I went to bed. I had to. I was only a couple of weeks into recovering from an emergency c-section, and the new-baby schedule was relentless. I was tired all the time and aware in every part of my being that this new state of affairs was permanent.

Permanent. Like a tombstone.

I lay in bed that night and cried. Cried from frustration and exhaustion but mostly because I had only been a mother for a few weeks and I already missed myself.

I was the girl who would stay up late and laugh at the consequences. I was the girl who chose friends over everything else. And most of all, I was the girl who never went through anything this hard alone.

Of course, I wasn't alone exactly. Nate was with me all the way, but I had told him a few days earlier that he could stop getting up in the middle of the night. All the baby wanted was to nurse before falling back asleep, and no one could do that but me. I figured if one of us got enough sleep, then at least we'd be half sane.

Wasn't I reasonable? Yes. Yes, I was. Reasonableness was the bedrock of my old self.

My new self, though, felt unexpected resentment about this decision I had made of my own free will. Not resentment aimed toward Nate (most of the time I wasn't that unfair), but a resentment aimed at the injustice of the world. This baby had changed my whole life, my whole body, my whole personality (or so it felt), and thanks to simple biology my husband got to go on as before.[1]

---

[1] This is the point where Nate smiles and says, "Being a man is awesome." Which I allow because a) I don't often get to win the "who deserves more pity" award, and b) he usually offers head rubs or ice cream runs to make up for all that I suffer.

By that point in my life, I had left my friends and family behind, moved across the world, and experienced the emptiness of a Christmas morning with nothing to greet me but unnatural sunshine. But none of these things had ever made me feel as lonely as lying in that bed listening to my friends laugh on the other side of the door. Because always before, Nate had been with me, experiencing what I was experiencing and understanding what I was feeling. And now, for the first time, something felt like it was happening to me alone.

And this baby was forever. So wasn't the loneliness forever, too?

I wish I could say that the next day I expressed all of my feelings and we talked until Nate understood me perfectly and then kept talking until I came to grips with this identity shift. In reality, though, I'm not good at feelings, and I had long before developed a neat little unspoken flowchart for dealing with negative emotions:

> Have them → briefly wallow in them → find them exhausting/embarrassing →push them away → forget about them → oh wait, are those pesky feelings back again?

I know, right? Not super healthy. But it was terrifically effective for getting things done.

The result, of course, was that it took me a long time to accept how much my life had changed now that I had a kid. You wouldn't think someone so tiny would have such huge demands, but every day I was discovering some new way she was shifting everything.

It helped when the baby began to need so much more than round-the-clock nursing that Nate experienced his own identity shift, putting us back on the same emotional plane. But I was slow to come to grips with what it meant to be a mom and even slower to figure out how I could be whatever that was and also be myself.

When Ellie was four months old, we returned to Argentina and our life's work. It felt good to be back in the routine, especially since the "routine" already involved constant adaptation, so the changes that came with the baby felt less jarring.

In overseas mission work, there are a million jobs to perform. Handyman, teacher, taxi driver, party planner, tour guide, nutritionist, counselor, translator, accountant. I loved learning how to do all those things. New challenges and new experiences are what I am all about. Now that I had added mom to the list, I was constantly looking for ways to integrate that with the other aspects of my job. Culturally, it was accepted that I'd bring my baby everywhere I went, so I was relieved to be able to do many of the things that made me feel normal.

Many but, of course, not all. Some things just weren't feasible while nursing an infant, as I discovered the week a friend asked Nate to preach at his nearby church.

By far, my favorite part of my job was public speaking. It wasn't a regular thing, but from time to time, Nate and I would be asked to teach at a youth camp or speak at church events, and even when it was in Spanish, I loved it. Maybe it's the teacher in my soul or maybe I just enjoyed attention, but I never felt more energized than when I could stand in front of people and communicate something that was important to me. Nate and I preferred to teach together. We had a rhythm and a combined energy that felt so good when it was working.

And now, once again, the baby was disrupting our rhythm. None of our local churches had nurseries where you could leave a baby (it would have been culturally weird). We didn't have grandparents nearby, and all our usual babysitters were...well, they were at church. So even though we had written the content of the message together, we agreed that Nate would have to take this one solo.

Theoretically, this should have been fine. Nate is an amazing speaker all on his own, and I had an infant who still didn't sleep through the night. I was exhausted and didn't need one more thing on my plate. I could have even stayed home that night. It was getting close to winter and the sun set early. The service would be late enough that I had every excuse to keep the baby inside and put her to bed at her normal time.

It's probably what a sane person would have done or, say, a person without the world's most advanced case of FOMO. All I could think was that I was already missing out on speaking up front. I shouldn't also have to miss out on being there.

So I went. And it was a little late for the baby. And hanging out with a bunch of people I didn't know very well proved to be more awkward than fun. And, of course, the minute Nate stood up to preach, Ellie started to cry.

She didn't want to nurse and she was never going to sleep in a room full of interesting new things. She also didn't want me to sit still or be inconspicuous in any way. I know I said that I like attention, but it turns out that I am somewhat picky about what kinds of attention I appreciate.

Desperate not to make any more of a scene, I slipped out the back door into the courtyard outside. It was a bit chilly, brisk enough that I was glad of my coat, but not cold enough to keep me from sweating inside that coat as I walked back and forth and bounced my baby up and down. I paced and I sweated and I grumbled in my mind about the unfairness of my being out here soothing this baby while my husband was inside doing something I loved.

I didn't blame Nate for where I was—it was my choice as much as his—but I have found that I can easily be mad without the need for blame. So I indulged my self-pitying anger for all it was worth. Once again, I let the moment grow in my mind, so that my situation represented the plight of women everywhere, overlooked and oppressed, all because we are biologically equipped to carry and nurse children.

After a while, I discovered that as long as I kept up a sort of swaying bounce, Ellie would settle down and stay quiet, so I had a new opportunity to build on the narrative of martyrdom I was spinning by creeping up close to the door to listen to Nate as he spoke. The window was open a crack, allowing me to hear, and slowly I eased closer and closer until my nose was nearly up against the glass.

I know. The symbolism of the moment was a little heavy-handed. I was literally outside, looking in at where I wanted to be, prevented from being there by the baby in my arms. If you saw this moment in a movie, you'd be like, "Geesh, no need to hit me over the head with it."

At that moment, though, I wasn't seeing the humor in the situation. Discontent had squeezed all perspective from my soul, and I wanted the metaphor to be so obvious that even the strangers in the room would have to see it.

They did not, of course. That's the thing about self-pity. No one else ever takes it as seriously as you do.

Again, I'd like to tell you that I had a revelation that night. That I looked down at my sweet daughter's face and realized that she was infinitely more wonderful than anything I loved doing, that I would have more impact on the world by raising her than by any amount of public teaching. I mean, those things are true, and on some level I knew that. This is the reason I chose to have kids in the first place. But I did not reach a new state of enlightenment that particular night. That night, I stood there and tortured myself with what I couldn't have and then went home in a dark, unfriendly mood.

Aren't I fun?

I was just a little girl when I first heard the story Jesus told about a seed. Maybe you've heard it, too.

A seed is just a kernel, but it holds the potential to grow into a strong, beautiful tree, to send roots down deep and branches up toward the sun, to give shelter to animals and shade to the weary. But the story of the seed starts in the ground, where, in order to become that miracle of a tree, the seed first has to die. It gets buried in the dirt and then literally falls apart. Its hard outer shell rots away. Then, and only then, does it begin to grow.

No one who wants to grow gets to escape dying. It's part of the deal, the only way through to the life we were meant to live. And still, every time we experience it, it feels like the worst thing that could happen to us.

I'll be honest. For me, becoming a mother was a kind of death. Absolutely a death that led to resurrection and new life—I wouldn't trade it for the world. But in the moment of death, you don't really feel happy about being made new, you know? You just feel miserable. You feel...like you're dying.

Dying hurts, and I was never any better with pain than I was with feelings.

Luckily, motherhood was going to give me all the practice I needed.

2

If Denial Is A River, I'm Building A Houseboat

Most of my early years as a mom were spent in Argentina. Nate and I moved to Buenos Aires at 25 with no children. When we moved home permanently at 34, we had three kids: Ellie was six, Scott was four, and Lucy was two. There's a lot to say about raising babies in a foreign country, and we'll get to that eventually, but for now, let's start with the weather.

Rain in Argentina meant two things, particularly in the last house we lived in. First, the ground water would rise, and there was the very real possibility that water would pour in under the front door or rise up through the floor drains to flood the house. Secondly, and more urgently, rain meant the laundry was in danger.

Clothes dryers didn't exist in our neighborhood so all clothes had to be dried on racks on the back patio, and by the time I had three small children, you'd better believe I had laundry out there every day of the week. That meant being on rain watch at all times. The climate was humid, and even under normal circumstances it was hard to get things dry before mildew set in. If a load got rain-soaked, we would all be going naked by the time I got caught up.[1]

One afternoon when my youngest, Lucy, was still a baby, I heard the first small slaps of rain against the window. Obviously, I dropped what I was doing and darted outside. I managed to drag both huge clothes racks inside before they were more than lightly sprinkled. Relieved, I was turning back to work when a motion made me stop.

The flapping wings caught the corner of my eye and they were big enough to draw my full attention. I watched as something the size of my fist rose up from the clothing racks, wings going full speed, darting toward the closed window.

A. Hummingbird. Was. In. My. Kitchen.

Obviously, I felt a brief panic and worry about how I was going to get it back outside, but both feelings were overwhelmed by the excitement of seeing a hummingbird up close. I instantly wanted to share this thrill with my children.

"Kids!" I yelled. "Come and see this!"

---

[1] I know I'm not really selling it, but I want to clarify that I loved my life in Argentina. When even a simple rainstorm makes you leap into action, you're living the whole adventure, you know? Weird as it may sound, this was exactly how I wanted my kids to grow up.

I was pretty sure that they had never seen a hummingbird before, so this was going to be a fun new discovery.

Their little feet were already pattering toward me when the creature landed on the window, wings stilling for a moment.

It. Was. Not. A. Hummingbird.

It was a moth. And with its wings stretched out on either side, it was as big as both my hands put together.

Sudden horror overtook me. I could not let my children see that moth! One look and they'd be having nightmares for a week.

"Never mind!" I called, stepping over to block the doorway and trying to keep my voice light. "Never mind! It wasn't what I thought!"

My son, Scott, turned away quickly, eager to get back to his toys, but five-year-old Ellie was not so easily deterred.

"What is it?"

"Nothing," I said, dancing sideways to block her view with my body. "No big deal."

She looked at me funny and tried to see past my body. I waited her out, my face a mask of disinterest. I don't think she believed me, but finally she shrugged and gave up.

Crisis averted, I sighed in relief. Now I just had to deal with a moth the size of a Mardi Gras mask and we'd be good.

I'll spare you the horrifying details.[2]

As soon as it was over, I flopped down in a chair to berate myself. What was wrong with me? Why did I think that thing was a hummingbird? Now that I was back in my right mind, I realized that never once in all my years in Argentina had I ever seen a hummingbird. For all I knew, there were no hummingbirds on the whole continent.[3] Moths, though, I had seen in plenty. Not to mention other flying insects, some of enormous size.

And yet, when a flying creature appeared in my kitchen, my first assumption was that it was a delightful little bird I should show my children.

I feel like that neatly summarizes my most basic natural instincts. If I'm not careful, in any given situation, I will see only what I want to see. And what I want to see is always something happy.

I'd love to call this optimism, but if I'm honest, it's really more like denial most of the time. And while denial may seem like an easy path, believe me, you have to work incredibly hard to maintain it. I would know. I was

---

[2] Suffice it to say that it would not "shoo" outside and I had to kill it. I had to kill a lot of critters over the years, and I'd gotten somewhat used to the necessity, but this one made me cringe. It was just so much like a bird.

[3] I've looked it up since. There are hummingbirds in South America, but they mostly live closer to the equator.

personally dedicated to ignoring anything painful for most of my childhood and teen years. Plenty of hard things happened, but I found that I didn't feel them as much if I just buried myself in books or in my own imagination and did my best to focus only on what was pleasant. They say denial is a river, so I built a houseboat, and I didn't just visit occasionally, I laid down carpets and added throw pillows to make it homey.

While not everyone is as inclined to avoidance as I am, I'm not the only one to drop anchor in that river. For those of us who live in relative comfort and luxury, it's soothing to believe our situation represents the real world. When you've never suffered, it's nice to believe you never will, and when you have, it feels safer to pretend it didn't matter.

Of course, you can't ignore the darkness forever. It has a way of reaching you no matter how hard you work to avoid it.

For me, it was having kids that forced me out of my cozy floating home. There just wasn't room for us all to be comfortable in there.

Early on in our parenting life—Ellie was not quite one—Nate and I were asked to take a short trip to Paraguay. Mentoring and encouraging people starting new churches in more remote places was a part of our job and, as with everything else, we believed that we did it best when we did it together. We knew things would be more complicated with a baby, but we didn't see any reason for that to stop us.

"No problem," I said. "We'll just take Ellie along. She loves to travel. And everyone loves babies."

There's such a fine line between being optimistic and being delusional, don't you think?

We asked our teammates about it. They had never done a trip like this with children, but they assured us that it was a short flight and that the family who would be hosting us would love to have our baby, too.

Those things were true, by the way. One hundred percent true. Also, I didn't ask nearly enough questions.

My first clue that I might have made a mistake came when we arrived at the house where we'd be staying. As promised, our hosts were delighted to see us and gushed over Ellie's beauty and charm, and then they showed us to our room to leave our bags. We were sleeping in their son's bedroom— he'd be staying at a friend's during our visit. The room didn't have a door. The only thing between us and the rest of the house was a brightly patterned curtain.

Instantly, I thought of how Ellie sometimes still woke up crying at night.

"It'll be fine," I told myself, "You'll just nurse her if she wakes up." I eyed the two twin beds where we'd be sleeping and even my optimism quailed a little at the thought of bringing her into bed with me. But after all, she often slept all night, and we'd had a tiring trip. Probably it wouldn't even be a problem.

It was the cold that did us in. Paraguay is a lot closer to the equator than Buenos Aires, so even though it was late winter, the days were warm and sunny, and it never occurred

18

to me that cold might be an issue. Until nighttime, when the temperature dropped like it had fallen off a cliff.

After about ten minutes of each sleeping in a bed with one blanket, Nate and I realized that we needed better heat conservation and squeezed into one single bed with both blankets on top. I was so grateful for those warm wool blankets. Even after they began to produce an allergic reaction.

Eyes and nose running, I pulled that scratchy mess up to my chin and fell asleep anyway…for about two hours. Then Ellie woke up.[4]

I nursed her, shivering and sniffling and sitting on the edge of the empty bed, then laid her down and went back to sleep. She woke again. I did the same. By her third waking, I was deranged with exhaustion and I attempted to bring her into the twin bed with us. I honestly can't remember the rest of the night other than a haze of cold and aches and itchy eyes and the vague fear that the baby would fall out of the bed.[5]

Morning was a huge relief. The family we were visiting was excited about this wonderful work they were doing in the local public school. They took us on a visit of every classroom. And the work *was* wonderful. It was inspiring

---

[4] I don't know if it was the cold or the unfamiliar place or just the perversity of infants, but she woke up at least four times every night that we were there.

[5] It's a miracle that she didn't.

and encouraging. Unfortunately, our ability to appreciate it was severely compromised by the gastrointestinal distress that reared its head right about the time we arrived at the school. We'd been eating too many unfamiliar foods, and so we spent the morning hopping back and forth from classrooms of eager schoolchildren to tiny inadequate bathrooms, tossing the baby back and forth between us like a hot potato.

We spent four days in Paraguay. Four days and three nights.

On the second night, I was dreading that bed so much, I almost cried. Ever resourceful, I wrapped an old t-shirt around the top of the blanket, so it didn't actually touch my face. It helped with the sniffling. Still, I lay there in the cold, unable to roll over on my sliver of bed, waiting for my baby to start crying, and cursed my earlier denial of reality. Who takes a baby on a four-day trip to an unknown situation in a third-world country? Who thinks that will be "no problem?"

In the middle of so much miserable reality, denial was no longer an option, so I tried out the alternatives. Depression. Bitterness. Cynicism.

For a long while in that uncomfortable bed, I reveled in self-loathing and misery, and then, after an hour or two, I suddenly found myself thinking out how I was going to describe this trip when I wrote to my friends. The baby's cries echoing through the night in the tiny house, the child-sized toilets in stalls with no doors at the school, the blankets that made me sneeze. The more I thought about explaining the trip, the more hilarious the trip seemed, and suddenly, right there in the middle of living it, I saw the upside of terrible mistakes. They make for amazing stories.

In the briefest moment of clarity, I saw the middle ground between denial and self-pitying cynicism, the place where you look your misery straight in the face and laugh at it.

I won't lie: I didn't sleep any better that night (or the night after) and I've never been so glad to leave a place.[6] I learned my lesson and made better arrangements when traveling with my children in the future. But none of those things took away from how much I enjoyed telling that story.

I let myself be honest about my unhappiness. I did not minimize how awful it was, but I also didn't beat myself up about it. I just laughed at myself.

And we've been laughing about it ever since.

---

[6] A sentiment my wonderful hosts did not deserve.

3

Shut Up And Enjoy This Magical Moment

A few years ago, we had the most charming Christmas morning. The kids woke up early, their stockings were stuffed with all their favorite things, and everyone got the donut they liked best. Our house was cozy, the tree was sparkling, and miraculous snow covered the ground outside. The only thing we needed, Nate declared, was a fire crackling away in the fireplace.

And then he sent the girls to get firewood and the boy to dump the ashes from the previous fire into the ash pile in the woods.

You should have seen their faces. It was like he had eaten all the Christmas cookies. Chores on Christmas morning? You can't ruin Christmas morning with chores!

Scott, my middle child and only son, was particularly furious. He wanted to refuse. He very badly wanted to refuse. But in our house, kids don't refuse to obey direct commands from parents. Instead, he put on his snow boots over bare feet. He slammed out the door. And he dumped the ashes in the middle of the back yard instead of going all the way to the woods.[1]

Needless to say, it was a little while before we could open any Christmas presents. First, we had to clean up the mess. Then, we had to take a few minutes to talk about how even on Christmas we all have to do our part because magic isn't actually effortless—magical days take just as much work as ordinary days, and usually more.

It was a hard conversation for me. I felt like I was lecturing myself. As much as Scott is like his dad, he inherited a few of my second-child qualities. To put it bluntly, the entitled little apple doesn't fall far from the entitled apple tree.

This is another of my many flaws that seemed so minor until my kids came along to amplify them. My imagination loves to create idyllic scenes, and when reality doesn't live up, I am less than charming about it.

Like, not even a little bit charming.[2]

One of my favorite ideals of parenting is that parents can expose kids to all the things we love, introducing them to art and culture and critical thinking at an early age. To a large extent, Nate and I have done this, and it's been

---

[1] The "woods" were located an extra ten feet away.

[2] Okay, yes; I'm a jerk.

24

awesome. But the reality of this ideal almost never looks the way I want.

If you see me with my now teenaged kids at a lecture on presidential history, you might be tempted toward admiration, but I urge you to take a minute to ask them about it. Ask about how many times someone was unbearably thirsty and all I did was hiss at them to be quiet. Ask about the unjust way I arbitrarily gave away the coveted seat next to me (somehow slighting every single one of them in the process) or the amount of times they've been bribed with ice cream into enduring similar boring outings. They've had some awesome experiences, but it isn't all smooth sailing.

There's a reason people don't take young children to art shows, you know? You can absolutely do it, but you'd better bring a lot of snacks and water and be prepared for embarrassing comments in unnecessarily loud voices.

In our case, though, the issue has been less about art shows and history lectures and more often about *Star Wars*.

Yes, *Star Wars*. The rise of geek culture and its increasing power in mainstream life has been one of the unexpected joys of my adulthood. I grew up in the eighties, the decade that produced dozens of movies about nerds being bullied by cool people with enormous hair, so I was pretty much planning to keep my love of sci-fi a secret forever.

But lo and behold, here we are in the 21st century, and my people are on top![3]

Nate and I were married the year that the *Star Wars* prequels began to come out, and our last baby entered the world around the same time Marvel started its quest to take over the universe. We have not hesitated to immerse our kids in all the things we love. Ellie was watching the original *Star Wars* movies before she could talk. A giant Bat Cave was one of Scott's first favorite toys. I began reading the Harry Potter books out loud to them as soon as they started school, and we took Lucy along to our family viewing of *The Hobbit* before she turned five.[4]

Lucy, more than anyone, has seen every new geek blockbuster at an age most people would still be thinking *Frozen* was too intense. I totally understand why people make other choices, but I don't regret taking Lucy to these movies as a young child. Yes, sometimes she was too little to hang with it all,[5] but she's been able to participate in shared family experiences and she now has

---

[3] Don't worry. I haven't let it go to my head. But I do buy nerdy Lego sets for myself sometimes, and I'm not even ashamed of it.

[4] It didn't hold her attention the whole time, but when we left, she happily told us the goblins were her favorite part.

[5] She famously fell asleep in the middle of *Rogue One* twice in one week. Because of course we saw it twice.

the language and context to evaluate storytelling at a level that's way beyond her age.

The downside is that for a long time her favorite part of movie-going was the popcorn and the giant fountain drink, which meant she had to be taken to the bathroom at least three times in every movie. And because she wasn't that invested in the plot, she didn't pick good moments to make her restroom requests. Important dialogue? "I need to pee!" Can it wait a moment? "No! Right now!"

Any reasonable person would realize that if you're going to take a child to a movie (or any event) that isn't really designed for her, you'll have to be patient and understanding as she reacts like a child who is at an event that isn't really designed for her. It's the trade-off you make for the benefits of being together as a family.

Did I say I was a reasonable person? Oops.

I really, really hated those bathroom trips. Not enough to leave her at home. Not enough to stop going to the movies. Just enough to be mean about it.

It was somewhat easier to be patient when she was small, but as she got older, my patience got thinner. I would try to restrict her drinking, but she would just interrupt the movie to complain about how thirsty she was. I would prepare her ahead of time to space out her drinking and hold off until the end, but these warnings had very little effect.

Everything came to a head when the movie *Solo* came out. I was hyped to see it as Han Solo had long being a central figure in my life. So were Nate and Ellie and Scott. Lucy was...well, Lucy was in a particularly uninterested-in-*Star-Wars* phase, for which we were all trying to forgive her. But she did want to go along and participate in the fun.

I gave her due warning in advance. I was very excited about this movie. I wanted to watch the whole thing. I wanted us to have a fun family event, uninterrupted by any whining or urgent needs to leave the theater. She was old enough that I really felt she should be able to last the whole movie, and I told her so.

The movie started, and it was going well, better than I had expected even. I began to hope that maybe Disney wasn't going to ruin Han Solo after all. We were having a great time as a family. Everyone was laughing and enjoying themselves, and then...Lucy had to pee.

Here's where my dark side goes on full display. I wasn't just annoyed. I was enraged. It's embarrassing to admit it because, yes, I do know that it's just a silly movie, but she was messing up my perfect moment, and I was so mad at her.

I told her we weren't going. Straight up no.

She didn't exactly whine, but she did repeat her request a few times. I hissed that I had warned her we weren't leaving and that she was ruining the movie and should just hold it.

You like my idea of family fun?

A little while later, it was clear that Lucy was actually in pain and that I had no choice but to take her. With very bad grace, I did. I hurried her out and back in, making sure to let her know what a huge inconvenience this was.

She sat through the rest of the movie quietly, and when it was over, she turned to me with tears in her eyes. Sweetly, she took my hand and apologized for needing the bathroom.

And finally, thank God, I melted.

What was wrong with me that I would make my daughter feel bad for needing something everyone needs sometimes? Why would I think a child should have the self-control many adults don't have just because otherwise she inconvenienced me? I mean, it's perfectly human to be annoyed at interruptions, but why would a kid acting like a normal kid be so enraging? After all, I was the one who took her to a place designed for me and not for her.

I apologized, we snuggled, and I promised myself I would do some hard thinking.

I have lived my life in search of perfect moments. The relaxing summer day, with nothing but a book, a gentle breeze in the shade, and ice in your glass that never seems to melt. A hike up a mountain with the perfect companion, arriving at stunning vistas just as the sun slants through the trees. That magical Christmas morning.

And to be perfect, it has to be *perfect*, you understand. No ugliness or discomfort can mar the beauty of the moment. No mosquitoes can buzz around my summer day, nor can phone calls interrupt my reading. No one can decide to sleep in on Christmas morning or cry that their hot chocolate burned their tongue. No blisters can distract from my hiking bliss, and no companion can talk about politics when we should be in quiet awe of the view. Just shut up and enjoy the magical moment, would you?[6]

Obviously, this is absurd. People weren't made for perfection. Life wasn't made for perfection. *I* wasn't made for perfection. I know this, but somehow it still makes me irrationally angry every time.

---

[6] This demand that other people live up to my obscure expectations isn't a new problem for me. On our first anniversary, Nate and I took a trip with my parents through Yellowstone, up over Bear Tooth Pass and into Montana. Nate had never been there before, and I was excited to show him the amazing view from the top of the pass. Unfortunately, the winding ride uphill in the backseat of a car, combined with the extreme altitude, made him sick. When we finally got to the top, he barely wanted to get out of the car to look around. My perfect moment was ruined, and instead of concern for my husband's well-being, all I felt was anger. In my frustration over not getting my one shining moment, I got surly and managed to ruin a whole day.

It's humbling to take an honest look at the arrogance that would insist that imperfection isn't good enough for me. It's ugly to admit that I value my own mental picture over the well-being of others. But I'll never be who I want to be until I speak the truth to myself. It's not whatever is happening around me that is ruining my happiness. It's my own selfishness that is doing that.

I might have happily ignored this truth forever, but thanks to my kids' relentless introduction of imperfection into my life, I get the chance to grow.

These days I'm trying to stop clinging to idyllic mental pictures and to start embracing the rougher beauty of reality. When I introduce my kids to something I love, I dial my expectations of their response down to low and let them experience it in their own way. If someone's sickness cancels Thanksgiving dinner, we celebrate on a different day. And when I go to the movies, I don't worry about catching every line. It'll make its way to a streaming service at some point.

And the little moments of perfection? They still come sometimes. They just come at unexpected moments and in ways I could never engineer.

They come on a random Tuesday, when Lucy suddenly wants to snuggle before school, and we get ten precious minutes on the couch, her head tucked under my chin, talking about life and the future.

They come when the kids want to carve pumpkins but I just can't take the mess, so I make them go outside, and they'll only agree if I'll read to them. The next thing I know I'm reading *The Lord of the Rings* out loud to my pumpkin-carving children while the sun sets on a beautiful fall day.

Perfect moments can't be predicted, they can't be forced, and they almost never come on holidays. They just happen, gifts to be delighted in, not rights to be demanded.

And in between, there's the magic of the imperfect moments. All the while I'm swatting mosquitos and cleaning up spilled milk and taking fourteen trips to the bathroom, I'm living life with the wonderful, imperfect people I love.

I just have to get over myself and embrace it.

4

The Wicked Witch Of The West Has Nothing On Me

My busy little bee of an oldest daughter was three years old when I first uttered what became one of my most-used parenting lines.

We were home from Argentina for a few months, living in a small town in Indiana and trying out normal life for a change. I had taken the kids out to the park to pick blackberries, the kind of little outing I invented on days that we didn't have scheduled activities for a preschooler who wanted to GO and DO. On our way home, it became clear that we had not GONE and DONE nearly enough.

"Where are we going now?" asked Ellie.

"We're taking our blackberries home."

"No! I want to go to Gaga's house!"[1]

"We can't go to Gaga's house. It's almost dinner time, and Gaga lives two hours away."

"No, she doesn't! She lives close! I want to go to Gaga's house!"

"Her house is two hours from here. That's four episodes of Dora. We have been in the car for five minutes, and Scott is already crying. We can't drive two hours tonight."

"No! She lives close! She lives close!"

This went on for a while, Ellie getting increasingly angry and me puzzling over how to make her understand time and distance.

Finally she shouted. "It's. Not. Two. Hours."

That's when I stopped the car, turned around, and said, "You can say that as many times as you like, but *you can't change reality.*"

Then I drove home, refusing to engage in the argument and trying to ignore her yelling.

---

[1] Gaga was the name we had settled on for Nate's mom, as it was the closest Ellie could get to Grandma when she was little.

Whoever said you should reason with small children never met any of my kids.

I can't tell you how many times over the years I've had to repeat a variation of "you can't change reality."

Seriously, the Wicked Witch of the West has nothing on me.

"I know you wish Saturday was tomorrow, but it's Thursday. Wishes won't change reality. We have no choice but to live through Friday first."

"I get that you really want apple juice, but we ran out of apple juice. There is no more apple juice in our house. I cannot make apple juice appear out of thin air. That's just reality."

What's infuriating is that these obviously salient points were never convincing to my children. What I've learned is that accepting reality is a two-part process. The first part is acknowledging what is real, but the second and far harder part is letting go of how you feel about it.

I did not figure this out quickly. In fact, it took me more than five years of parenting to accept the reality of my children's difficulty accepting reality, and I can still remember the day I realized I needed to let it go.

Ellie was five and bitterly furious with me. I may be remembering it wrong (there were just so many rages to keep track of) but as I recall, she wanted to watch another episode of her favorite TV show and I said no.

"Why not?" she whined.

"Because you've already watched TV for the last hour, and that's enough TV for one afternoon."

"But there's nothing else to do!"

"There's lots to do. Read your books, play with your toys, color."

"Can we go to the park?"

"No, Lucy is sleeping."

"Then why can't I watch another show?"

"Because too much TV is bad for kids' brains."

"It's not bad for my brain!"

"It's not bad when you watch a little bit, but it's not healthy to watch too much."

"It's not too much! It's just one more!"

"You've already watched two."

"Just one more!"

"No."

By now, she was yelling. "You are so mean!"

"I'm not mean. I'm doing what I think is best for you. And you are throwing a fit. That won't get you anything. You need to go to your room."

Because she was five and had at least learned the consequences of direct disobedience, she went. She loudly decried my horrible unfairness as she went, but she went.

Trying to calm myself, I went to the living room and read a book to Scott while Ellie stayed in her room, slowly ratcheting down from furious yelling tears to an unintelligible mumble. When it was finally quiet from her direction, I took a deep breath, left my son with his toys, and went to see if she was ready to apologize for her fit and move on. As I put a hand on the doorknob, I could hear her talking quietly to herself inside the room. I leaned my head in to listen.

"She is so mean. She never lets me do anything. She always says no, and there's nothing else to do. She just doesn't care..."

It was a low-key rant on repeat, and you guys, everything she was saying was so unfair that I was instantly angry. I made one perfectly justifiable decision and now my daughter was convincing herself I was the wicked witch of the west. It was like hearing a friend tell lies about me behind my back. I wanted so badly to justify myself. I wanted to burst in there and set her straight, to force her to admit that I was a wonderful mother. I pictured exactly what I would say. I'd give her all the good, logical reasons for my decision. There would be science to back it up and the example of other parents she knew. I'd remind her of all the fun things we did all the time. I'd explain what I would be like if I were actually mean and tell her how lucky she was that I'm not like that.

It would have been a masterpiece of persuasive rhetoric.

It would have helped nothing.[2]

Luckily, just before flinging the door wide and letting loose, I realized what I was doing. Not only was trying to make a five-year-old understand me a losing battle, it wasn't even the right fight. My daughter didn't need to be educated or convinced. She knew the truth. She just didn't like it. And there, in the quiet of her room where it was hurting no one, she was venting her anger at things not going her way.

How many times have I needed the space to do that?

Quietly, I stepped away from the door, thinking about a particular afternoon when Ellie was a baby.

She had always struggled with naps. I was tired all the time and convinced that all those well-meaning people who told me to sleep when she slept were idiots. Many naps, she didn't sleep more than 20 minutes, so even if I threw myself into bed as soon as she drifted off, I'd barely be asleep before she was waking up again. On one

---

[2] I know because I had tried it. Too many times.

particularly bad day, I dragged myself through the morning, and when I finally succeeded in getting Ellie to sleep, I lay down on my own bed and literally begged God to make this nap last at least an hour. Speaking out loud just to be sure I'd be heard, I told him that since he is supposed to know everything, he should know how much I needed sleep, and if he really loved me as he said he did, he would let me have this nap.

Fifteen minutes later, Ellie started to cry.

I cannot describe to you the rage that flowed through me. Rage against a God who claimed to care about me and yet couldn't give me just one small respite. Gritting my teeth, I rolled out of bed to get my baby and swore that when I died from lack of sleep, I'd spend my first weeks in heaven letting God know exactly how badly he'd mismanaged my life.

Sometimes, perspective isn't possible. Sometimes we just want reality to be different so badly that we can't listen to reason. Sometimes we have to mutter under our breath that life is so unfair and no one understands us. Sometimes muttering isn't loud enough, so we yell a few insults for good measure.

And then we come out of our rooms. We get out the play dough and we find ways to be happy without getting what we want. Most importantly, we keep living in the security and love of the very person we just grumbled against. Because the reality of that love can't be changed no matter how many times we say it isn't there.

My kids have called me mean a hundred times over the years. Sometimes I laugh and say, "Yep, I'm the meanest," because they hate that, and it's funny. The rest of the time, I say nothing.

We all know the truth. They live in my love every day.

I have nothing to prove.

5

Sorry If God's Gift Wasn't The One You Asked For

I am not a detail-oriented person.

That's the way I prefer to describe it. I suppose it would also be possible to say that I don't pay close attention to what's happening around me, that I forget important pieces of data, that I prefer to put off all boring routine tasks until forced to do them, and that I'm a bit of a slob. If you wanted to be ~~accurate~~ technical about it.

The bottom line is that I'm the woman who forgets to turn the oven off when I take the cookies out and who throws the clothes in the washer willy nilly without checking the pockets. It's a wonder I've survived being a parent this long.

As you may have noticed, parenthood involves a lot of details.

Everyone has to be fed multiple times a day, which not only means that food must be bought, prepared, and served, but also that thought must be taken for what will be nutritious and what you can actually get each person to eat. Everyone has to be clothed, which means knowing what size people wear, what level of scratchiness they will tolerate, what they have worn out or outgrown, and also maybe noticing what the weather is outside so that people can be dressed in the appropriate length of sleeves and pants. Don't get me started on hats and gloves. Or socks and shoes. Or sunscreen.

Then they get schedules. School and sports and music and friends. Practices and field trips and concerts and games. Backpacks and ball gloves and permission slips and book fair money.

I'll stop now. Suffice it to say, motherhood has provided me with the opportunity to improve myself.

And I've worked hard at it. I keep a shared online calendar and update it meticulously. I make weekly meal plans and grocery lists and I stick to them. I keep an umbrella and some sunscreen in my car at all times. I sign forms the minute I get them and send them back immediately so I can't forget them. I make To-Do lists for each day and I check them off. I write things down so I don't forget them.[1]

---

[1] Call about Ellie's orthodontist bill. Email Lucy's teacher about science fair. Make Scott's doctor appointment. Text Jack's mom about Friday. Buy snacks for practice.

So yeah, I'm proud of my organization. Twenty-five-year-old me would be astonished.

Lest you think I'm bragging, though, let me tell you a story.

Once the kids started school, I began to write full-time, so I was home alone during the day. One beautiful fall day several years ago, I was wrapping up a morning of writing, sitting on my back patio in the sun, feeling very good about my life, when my phone rang.

Caller ID told me it was the school nurse, a call I always take for obvious reasons. I answered, mentally shuffling around my afternoon to include a sick child.

But the first thing she said was that everyone was fine.

Okay...

She was just calling because she had been walking through the cafeteria at lunch time, and she happened to notice that my son's shoes had massive holes in them. She just wanted to let me know that the school offers financial assistance for families for things like shoes if that's something that would be helpful.

Cue my stuttering humiliation.

Oh. Thanks for bringing that to my attention. No, financial assistance isn't necessary. I was planning to buy him new shoes, just didn't realize how urgent it was. I'll get him new shoes today. He'll be wearing them tomorrow. Thanks so much for calling. I really appreciate your concern.

You guys.

I knew my son needed new shoes. I knew they were wearing out. But I had no idea that they had giant holes in them. Because I did not ever, ever look closely at my son's shoes. From the moment he learned to put them on himself, I stopped paying attention. And my kindergarten son, also not interested in details or overly concerned with social niceties, never mentioned the giant holes. So I was sending him to school every day in shoes so raggedy that people assumed I couldn't afford new ones.

So much for my pride in being on top of things.

Obviously, I bought him new shoes. And he wasn't the slightest bit embarrassed, so no scars were left on his psyche. The next year, he changed schools, and in the big picture of things, that was just one little uncomfortable moment.

Cut to two years later. I'm at home, writing in my little library, and I get a call from the school nurse at my son's new school. He's a man, and this conversation is much more awkward than the last one.

No one's sick, nothing like that. He's just calling to tell me that my son's shoes stink really badly. So badly that "it's causing a disturbance in the classroom." (Yes, those were his exact words.) He just wants me to know that my son will need new shoes, but that financial assistance is available if we need it.

No, I'm not joking about this.

Once again, I thanked the man for bringing this to my attention. I assured him I would take care of it. I grabbed my purse and went to buy shoes.

This time, I was beyond angry with myself. How had this actually happened twice? How did I not learn from my previous mistake? I was sure my inattention as a mother had now caused permanent scars for my son. His shoes smelled so bad that it disrupted the classroom? He'd probably been mocked and was now labeled Stinky Shoe Kid, a nickname that would stick with him through high school and be the central pillar of the bullying he would receive. All because his mother JUST NEVER PAID ENOUGH ATTENTION TO NOTICE HIS DISGUSTING FOOTWEAR.

I worried about my son's utter humiliation all afternoon until he got home and I could gently ask him how he was doing. He didn't even understand my question. As it turned out, it was just the teacher who reported it. Apparently, his second-grade classmates were equally oblivious to horrible smells and my son was blissfully unaware of his social gaffe.

As my mom always used to say, it all worked out. It always does.

Even so, to this day I cringe inside when I think about those phone calls. My failure as a mother is stamped on my heart. Because that's most definitely how it felt to me, like I had failed the most basic level of motherhood.

It may have worked out, but it was pure luck that it did. This was something that I was meant to take care of, and I didn't. Something other adults noticed and had to act on because I hadn't. Something that could very easily have caused my kid humiliation.

For all my hard work to improve myself, my parenting has been full of these kinds of failures. I snap when patience would have served me better. I set a bad example with what I eat. I say I'm going to pick them up and then lose track of time.

I don't make a point of calling those things failures because I want to heap shame on myself and then walk around feeling awful. I believe that we should all be gracious to ourselves and others. But I can't give myself grace until I admit that I need it. I call my failures what they are because I need to acknowledge that I'm no better than anyone else and that I don't have to be.

I do fail, I mess things up, and my flaws cause pain for other people. There, I said it.

And I'm still okay.

I'm a mom and I'm also a human. This is life. It's complicated and messy, and everyone screws up. When I get something right, my kids benefit from my good

46

example. When I get something wrong, my kids get to learn valuable lessons about grace and forgiveness. When I cover all their needs seamlessly, they experience peace and harmony. When I drop some balls, they learn to step up and deal with it. And when, worst of all, I introduce real pain into their lives, they have a chance to develop the kind of resilience we all need in order to survive.

My kids, even with all their flaws and failures, are one of God's greatest gifts to me. So why can't I accept that I, even with all my flaws and failures, am one of his greatest gifts to them?

Can I tell you what I wish I could tell the Deb that took those phone calls years ago? You are the mom your kids were meant to have. You are God's gift to them, even if it wasn't the one they asked for.

You, the disorganized hot mess. You, the uptight stress ball. You, the loud-mouth, and also you, the wallflower.

Absolutely be the best you that you can be. But by definition, that means being YOU.

You get to be yourself!

Yourself is the one who made and/or chose these little darlings, and yourself is the one working hard to do right by them. Yourself is making difficult choices every day and doing the best you can.

And if yourself sometimes ruins small but expensive electronic devices in the washing machine because you never remember to check the dang pockets, well, it will all work out.

It always does.

6

All You Can Do Is All You Can Do, And All You Can Do Is Enough

As soon as I found out that I was having my first baby, I began to dream about what kind of nursery she would have.

We lived at the time in a cavernous upstairs apartment in one of the poorest neighborhoods in south Buenos Aires. The view from my iron-barred windows was dirt streets and cinderblock houses, overgrown lots and rusty metal baskets on high poles to keep the trash out of reach of the street dogs. I loved my life, and I'd never worried too much about the bleak surroundings, but this was going to be my baby's home. I wanted to make a place of beauty inside that bare, chilly apartment. I wanted to create an oasis of familiar comfort in a foreign land.

I worked hard through my pregnancy to turn that ugly bedroom into something magical. It took a lot of imagination. I started on a ladder (not my smartest move, maybe), hot-gluing blue fabric to the ceiling and then hanging little Christmas-ornament stars so it would look like the night sky. I painted the walls forest green. I had a friend take photos of pretty places near where our family lived and I framed them to hang over the changing table. I dragged in a wooden bookshelf to fill with books, and we bought a rocking chair to sit next to it. By any modern social media standards, the room was ridiculous, but in that place and time, it felt like a small miracle.

The nursery served its purpose. We went home to the US for Ellie's birth, and when we came back four months later, it was comforting to move her into that well-loved space. At least until reality set in.

At first, Ellie didn't want to sleep in there (or sleep alone ever, as it turned out). When she did, I discovered that the summer humidity was making all that fabric unstick from the ceiling and sag weirdly. Despite my best efforts, eventually the fabric and the stars fell down.

Then Ellie learned to pull herself up and wanted to climb out of her sweet white wooden crib. We discovered the worst drawback of her room one naptime, when she toppled over the edge of the crib and smacked her head on the hard tile floors, biting her tongue hard enough to leave a scar. Carpet was out of the question, so the crib had to go, replaced by an ugly but low-to-the-ground Pack 'n Play.

I had tried to create an illusion, but we still lived where we lived, and I was forced to admit that some things are beyond transformation.

Eventually, I accepted the reality of Ellie's bedroom, but I was still determined not to make any more concessions to my ideal family life than were absolutely necessary.

We had chosen our neighborhood intentionally, and we worked hard to make a difference there. We welcomed kids into our apartment to tutor them and to play games. We held movie nights and nutrition workshops in the plaza. We handed out school supplies and groceries. We gathered groups of men and women together to read about Jesus and sing and learn to love one another. We went to the hospital when people got sick, and we held parents' hands when they cried with worry about their children. People died, and we cried alongside those they had left behind.

We saw some beautiful miracles there: lives transformed by the power of God, fathers restored to their families, children continuing their education where it had seemed impossible, people with next to nothing caring for people with nothing at all. But we also learned that we could lavish every last drop of our love on our neighbors, and it would make only the smallest impact on their lives, if any at all. No matter how much we gave and talked and listened and taught, teenagers would still announce their pregnancy, children would still die of preventable accidents, husbands would still get drunk and abuse their wives. Maybe one less. Maybe for a while. But the oppressive hand of poverty could only be lifted so far, for so long.

Ellie and Scott were both born while we lived in that cinderblock apartment and worked in that wonderful, impossible neighborhood. Those were difficult years. I loved my work and found it painful to scale back as my kids took more and more of my time. I was exhausted and, for the first time in my life, sometimes truly depressed.

I just couldn't bring myself to give any of it up. I'd begun to let go of denial, and since I couldn't ignore the dark, I wanted to fight it with everything in me. I've always been competitive. I didn't plan to fight and not win. My friends and now my kids were depending on me. I was responsible to keep them safe from the darkness, and how better to do that than by defeating it?

I threw myself into work with the unconscious belief that if I could be perfect, could make all the right choices, could light as many fires as possible and shine as brightly as anyone has ever shone in the history of the world, I could carve out a place for my loved ones where no darkness could enter.

I tried. And I tried. And I tried. But every time, the darkness crept in around the edges. Or flooded in and made shadows where they shouldn't be. Or stomped in and suffocated lights I thought I could count on. And I didn't want to give up, I really didn't. But I just got so terribly exhausted.

Near the end of our time in that apartment, a man from our mission came to visit and after sharing some important things I've now forgotten, he looked around the table at our coworkers, locking eyes with each of us as he said, "All you can do is all you can do. And all you can do is enough."

Yes, we all nodded. Wise words.

"No," he said, "hear me. Hear me because I think in your hearts you don't really believe it. All you can do is all you can do. And all you can do is enough."

He was right. I didn't really believe it.

I wanted to. I longed to believe that I could stop trying to make things happen perfectly, that it would be okay, that I wouldn't be a failure. But after all, how could I know when I was really doing all I could do? And how could I ever be sure that it was enough?

So I worked on. I lit more fires and tried frantically to keep them from being extinguished.

But it was beyond me.

Over the next years, my own powerlessness would be thrown in my face over and over again. A combination of one key leader betraying the trust of the group and another being killed in a tragic accident eventually led to the scattering of that little community we had built. Nate and I went away, regrouped, and came back to another neighborhood in a nearby city with another team, this one built of people we trusted like family. We had Lucy with us by then, too, and for a few years, we poured ourselves into building up a new community. Once again, we saw miracles and we saw what a long and impossible journey stretched ahead of us. And then, once again, our little team fell apart and we had to leave the people we had come to love, conceding defeat. We packed up all three kids and moved back to the U.S. We started a new life. Again.

And I struggled to find a way to still be that person who built shining fortresses, even in the face of so much evidence that I couldn't make them last.

"All you can do is all you can do. And all you can do is enough." Those words haunted me as I did the seemingly insignificant and selfish work of caring for my own small family and not much more.

Those words echoed when my kids wanted to rake a maze

out of the leaves in the backyard, or make cookies, or help me wash the windows. I put the rake and the spoon and the spray bottle in their hands, and they did all that they could do. It was a small amount, a kid amount, but still, at the end of the day, we ran through a maze and munched on cookies as we stared at the trees through clean windows. Because I was the mom, and I made sure it turned out the way it was supposed to.

I thought about what it meant to be a parent, and the echo of that wise man's words felt a little less ghostly.

Here's the thing, and I really don't want to say this. It is the truth that I like the least, but it remains the truth in blatant disregard of my feelings:

I am not a superhero.

I am not a unique snowflake, capable of anything I put my mind to. I am not an earth goddess. I am a woman with a set number of hours to live each day, a limited supply of emotional and physical energy, and an absolutely normal tendency to make mistakes.

In the face of a world full of pain, I am never, ever going to have the answers. I am never going to drive out all the darkness.

All I can do is all I can do. And it isn't nearly enough.

Except that it is.

Because I am not alone. Because defeating the darkness is not my job. It's my Father's.

There it is. The thing that changes everything.

Can you imagine the relief of laying down a burden that was made for the God of the universe? Or the joy of finding that now that I know the battle doesn't rise or fall on my actions, I have more passion than ever for the fight?

Once I believe, really believe, that I'm not the most important character in this epic story of good versus evil, I can fight without the weight of the world holding me back. I can tend my fires, not out of desperation, but for the sheer joy of the light. After all, if I'm going to depend on an all-powerful God to do what I can't do, it doesn't matter how much or how little my part is. His infinite supply does not require my support.

I do what I can do, and I let that be enough.

It is enough already.

It is enough.

Part 2

Laughing With My Family

7

Why Don't You Come Over Here And Cherish This For Me?

I. Love. Holidays.

I always have.

I was lucky enough to have the kind of happy childhood that didn't leave scarring memories to ruin family celebrations, and I am wired to be on the lookout for the next reason to party.[1] So if there's a holiday, I'm here to bake something for it, and having kids only made my festive mania more manic.

One of the weird side effects of living in the southern hemisphere, where all the seasons are backwards, is that over time I developed a visceral longing for the changing of seasons and for holidays that felt like they should. I cooked giant turkeys and pumpkin pies on Thanksgiving, even though it was a million degrees in late November,

---

[1] Enneagram 7 if you care about such things.

every dish had to be made from scratch, and none of my neighbors had ever heard of the squash called pumpkin.[2] In April, I made homemade Easter egg dye and had my family send jellybeans, so we could pretend for a week that fall was actually spring.

Christmas was the craziest, though. We would start celebrating it as soon as Thanksgiving ended. I've been collecting advent calendars since I was a kid, and every year, I would hang them on the wall and open each one of those fun little doors. We would decorate the house with shiny bulbs and fake snow and a manger scene that the kids could play with. I'd play Christmas music every morning.

And then, when Ellie and Scott were five and three, and little Lucy had just started to crawl, I read about people who made a paper chain with a fun Christmas activity written on each link for each day of advent.

This was genius. It was magical. It was homemade. It was fun for all ages. I had to do it.

We celebrated the tinsel out of Christmas. That year and all the years after. We made up Christmas stories and sang Christmas songs. We wrote Christmas books and baked Christmas cookies. We did Christmas crafts and

_____

[2] Let the record show that, like a good hipster, I was in love with fall before being in love with fall was cool and that I had never even heard of pumpkin spice lattes.

put on Christmas plays. As they got bigger, I started worrying that we were making Christmas too much about ourselves, so we mixed in acts of kindness and service for others, babysitting for families with small children or taking cookies to neighbors or writing notes to those who needed encouragement.

During these Christmas golden years, Pinterest rose up to spur me on. Do you know how many cute advent calendar ideas are on Pinterest? We graduated from paper chains to paper Christmas trees to garlands to boxes. Every year, the kids looked forward to December 1 and the unveiling of the advent scheme.

It wasn't always easy to maintain. One of the greatest crises of my adult life broke loose one year in the last week of November. It was all-consuming for a while, and I remember walking in the door after another horrible day and realizing it was November 30. My sweet kids would be waking up the next morning expecting their yearly advent reveal, and I had nothing but a couple of bags of candy and the certain knowledge that it was impossible to plan what we'd we do the next day, much less for a whole month. But they were not yet ready to let go of that tradition, and in my state of grief, neither was I.

Late at night, sick at heart, I sat in front of the TV, dropping cherry cordial Hershey kisses into tiny advent boxes, eating at least one for every one I added to the calendar. I cut some tiny slips of paper and wrote on only two of them, not able to risk more of a promise than that we could watch a Christmas movie one day and read a Christmas story the next. I would continue to add activities one or two days at a time throughout that long, dark month.

For that year, the comfort of the tradition was worth the cost of stress added by trying to stay one step ahead of the passing days. It was a scattering of bright normalcy in the middle of chaos.

And then a few years later, in a perfectly ordinary and happy December, our tradition fizzled.

As always, I had made a plan and made a garland, and then it turned out that life had moved on. Sure, the kids were happy to see it on the first day. But as the days went by, sometimes we would open up our little activity and then never do it. Some days, we never opened it at all. It wasn't a lack of Christmas spirit; it was just homework and friends and increasingly diverse interests and, well, we were all just outgrowing it.

The next year in late November, remembering the year before, I asked the kids if they'd be disappointed if we didn't have an activity advent calendar. They all said it was totally fine. I was relieved and disappointed at the same time.

I wasn't alone. A few days later Scott came to me and said, "I'm actually sad that we aren't doing the advent calendar, but I also don't really want to do it. You know?"

It was growing up, summarized in one sentence.

Everything has its season. There's a time for everything. Christmas is here and then it's gone. Summer comes and then it goes. Your children are wide-eyed preschoolers and then they're teenagers and then they're adults. Your house is full of glitter and playdough and then it's full of books and cleats and then it's—I assume, someday—clean.

"Cherish each moment," people always say. "It goes by so fast." It does, for sure. Nothing lasts forever.

But I've always had quite a few questions for those givers of sage advice. How exactly do you know if you're cherishing the moment? Do you feel warm and uplifted in your heart? And what about the moments when you're changing a nasty diaper or being yelled at by a small irrational human or stepping on a Lego? If you are cherishing those moments, isn't that a form of mental illness?[3]

I deeply appreciate the perspective of age and have been blessed by those who remind me in the hardest times that "this too shall pass." But I have not found it possible to be fully aware at every moment of how fleeting my current season of life is. It's not realistic to insist that I see hard things as blessings and don't dare be unhappy for even a moment because in comparison to other seasons I have it so very good. Trying to manufacture

---

[3] Confession: sometimes when a well-meaning grandmotherly sort would look at my frazzled new mom face and tell me to cherish these moments, I would fantasize about saving my kids' next poopy diaper and delivering it to her with a little gift tag that said "Cherish this!" I might have a problem.

that kind of zen has added more stress to my life than it ever helped.

And honestly, why would I even want such a desperate, comparative happiness? If I'm not supposed to compare my life to other people's lives, why would I want to compare my life to my future or past life? How is that helping me now?

So here's my confession: I don't believe in cherishing every moment. It's too much pressure, and frankly, the word "cherish" is kind of weird.

I'd rather live enjoying each season of my life.

Because every season has its own joys, even if you have to look hard to find them, and every season has its own pains, even if other people tell you they aren't real. I've never found peace trying to ignore the pains and focus only on the joys. I've found peace when I embrace the joy and the pain as two sides of the same coin. When I hate the awful moments and love the wonderful moments and stop fretting about whether I used to have more of the one in the past or will have less of the other in the future.

Live now. Take what you have, the good and the bad.

And when the time comes, let it go. The good and the bad. Because a whole new set of good and bad is coming your way.

My kids don't write hilarious Christmas stories anymore, and even if they would let me video them singing Christmas songs, they no longer have those adorable lisps. They don't play with the pieces of the nativity set like they were action figures. But now their help with the Christmas cookies is actually helpful, and they catch my eye at family gatherings and share a knowing smile that makes light of the tension in the room. Now they buy me for-real Christmas presents with their own hard-earned money.

They're growing up.

And I guess if they are, I can, too.

8

Rage Monsters
Are People, Too

As I write these words, my oldest daughter is fifteen. If you met Ellie today, you'd be impressed by her maturity. She's smart and funny and responsible and kind. She'll play with your little children and talk to you about stories and softball and social justice. She's easily one of my favorite people.

I often wish that I could visit myself thirteen years ago and tell me about this Ellie.

Ellie thirteen years ago was a whole different experience.

She was the prettiest, sparkliest two-year-old you can imagine. The girl glowed with personality. Her smile lit up any room. She was also a wild roller-coaster of emotions that included a terrifying hundred-foot drop in the form of a rage that would take her over and turn her into an unrecognizable monster.

I'm not kidding. More than once I seriously wondered if my beautiful little girl was possessed by a demon.

I distinctly remember the first time I had that thought. Ellie had just turned one and still wasn't speaking any clear words. We had a friend over, a single guy, and we'd been enjoying a good visit while she napped. Then she woke up.

Sleeping had often been difficult with Ellie. It wasn't that she didn't sleep; it was just that she didn't ever want to be alone. Crazy American that I am, I wanted her to sleep in her own room, which meant that she cried herself to sleep at literally every nap and bedtime. Every. Single. One. She also woke up grumpy, but as an infant, it had been pretty easy to fix by feeding her and holding her for a while.

Not that day. That day, she woke up screaming, and nothing would do. I held her. She screamed. I put her down. She screamed. I gave her to Nate. She screamed. I offered her food. She screamed. I offered her juice. She screamed. I gave her a toy. She screamed. I sang her a song. She screamed. I soothed her reassuringly. She screamed. I sternly told her to stop screaming. She screamed. I held her. She screamed. I put her down. She screamed.

Am I repeating myself? Yeah. I tried everything twice. At least.

Our kind friend looked on in pity and horror as Nate and I finally put her back into her crib to scream in a safe place until she was done screaming. It took a long time.

And so I met Rage Monster Ellie for the first time.

Rage Ellie became a regular visitor at our house. Sometimes we could tell it was a result of being over-tired or hungry. Other times, we couldn't begin to imagine what brought it on. Sometimes she even woke up screaming in the middle of the night. Whoever named them night terrors must have been having a different experience because ours were night rages.

It was a lot to handle, and most days I felt like I was a horrible failure of a mother. Especially when it happened in public.

Because it did. All the time.

Most memorable was the day we were at McDonalds with a large group of friends. We frequented McDonalds in those days, partially for the taste of home and partially because we were the only ones with little kids and there was a play place to keep them busy while we talked with other adults. We could buy Ellie a happy meal with chicken nuggets and a tiny Sprite, and she'd be good for an hour, running back and forth between bites and sips and giant plastic tubes and slides.

On this particular day, when it was time to leave, she wasn't ready to go. The place was crowded, and she'd made a little friend, and she wanted to have another turn on the slide. One last turn, we said. But when the last turn was over, she wanted more. We said no.

Enter Rage Monster.

During her "last turn" we had packed up all our things. (You know, all the things you carry just to go out to lunch because you have a baby and a preschooler?) Nate was carrying Scott and a bag, and I had grabbed the remains of Ellie's lunch to feed her in the car. So now our hands were full, and our two-year-old was screaming and also bolting back toward the play place in complete defiance.

I sprang after her and performed one of those miracles of motherhood where you hold two things in one hand and still somehow grasp the arm of a writhing child. With much wrestling, I picked her up just before she disappeared inside a space too small for me to follow. She was loud in expressing her disapproval, and the entire McDonalds was staring.

"You can have your Sprite as we go to the car," I said.[1]

She grabbed the Sprite I offered, but instead of putting the straw in her mouth and effectively being silenced, she gave another yell of rage and hurled it into the play place. Even then, she had a good arm. It sailed through the tiny round opening dead center and smashed against the plastic bubble windows, flinging ice and sugar water all over the children inside.

---

[1] We can talk later about the fact that I was giving my two-year-old Sprite. For now, let's just say that my pediatrician in Argentina actually recommended giving it to her when she was six months old. Culture, man.

Humiliated, I held her even closer, reminding her through gritted teeth that consequences would be coming when we got to the car. It was hard to get the words out since it now took two hands to keep the writhing beast in my arms from falling to the floor.

Nate had gone to get a manager and some napkins to deal with our mess. He returned just in time to see our sweet blonde cherub rear her head back, open her mouth like a shrieking eel, and bite me hard on the chin.

In one move, Nate handed me the baby and took Ellie, slinging her raging self over his shoulder, and carrying her out of the McDonalds, through the food court,[2] and into the parking lot. I trailed behind with the bags and the baby, fighting back tears of pain and humiliation.

Ellie screamed the whole way.

I have distinct memories from my childhood of being in public and seeing kids throw tantrums. "There's a child who needs a spanking," my parents said, shaking their heads. "It's the parents' fault. Parents need to discipline their children."

Those memories ran through my head every single time I was dealing with Rage Ellie. I was trying to discipline her. We never let her get what she wanted by throwing a fit.

---

[2] Did I not mention this McDonalds was in a food court? Extra witnesses!

There were always immediate consequences for defiant behavior. We worked hard to be consistent. Lest you think my parents are harsh, please understand that I always felt very loved. I followed principles they taught me, and they were very good and effective. What I somehow didn't understand, though, is that with the particularly hard-headed and emotionally intense, you have to discipline consistently FOR YEARS before it has the intended effect. In the meantime, you are fodder for public judgment on a regular basis, and there is literally nothing you can do to stop it.[3]

When she was three and a half, still defiantly refusing to be fully potty trained and escalating huge fits at every afternoon "rest" time, I threw myself on the couch one night and told Nate, "This isn't working. I am literally disciplining her forty times a day, and I've been doing this for more than two years now, and it is having NO effect on her at all. We have to find some other method, some trick, some something."

"I don't think there is anything," he said. "I think we just have to keep doing the same things for as long as it takes."

He was right.

---

[3] I know some of you are thinking, "Well, you could..." Nope. Tried that. She raged anyway.

At around four years old, she turned a corner, and the rages started to decrease. We still had them, but instead of multiple times a day, they would only be once a day, then once every few days, then once every couple of weeks. She started preschool, and her little extroverted self was happier. We still had some sleep trouble and one memorable multi-hour battle after her baby sister was born, but sometimes a whole month would go by with no meltdowns.

Slowly, ever so slowly, she learned self-control. When she was seven, she came to me after a rage, and for the first time, she apologized for her behavior all on her own. I cried. When she was ten, we had our last massive head-to-head battle, which resulted in her being grounded from electronics for a month. She not only apologized once she had cooled down, she also complied with the rules of her grounding without a single complaint for weeks.

My girl still has a temper. Her emotions still cloud her judgment from time to time. But she continues to be herself when she's angry now. I haven't seen the Rage Monster in years.

I offer this story as a story of hope. Sweet mother of a raging two-year-old, this will not last forever.

But this is also a story of endurance. Ten years sounds short when you're reading it on a page, but each of those years had three hundred and sixty-five days in them, and each day had twenty-four hours, and yes, I'm counting the night time. I earned it. When 363 of your 365 days are spent battling a rage monster, it feels like time is crawling. And while you hope things will get better when they're five, you don't know that they will. For my son, five was when things started to ramp up. For my baby it was nine. Surprise!

I can't promise you it will get more peaceful at a later stage. While it hasn't been our experience yet, for many, the rages come back in full force in the preteen or teen years. And then there's an adult-sized human yelling at you irrationally, and you have a few more years to be loving and firm and consistent and wait helplessly for those things to have an effect.

This parenting thing is not a race. It's not even a marathon. It's one of those ultra-endurance-tough-mudder things you read about. You have to keep going and keep going and you never know when you'll turn a corner and be forced to crawl in mud or climb a wall instead of running.

Take heart. This will not last forever.

But it may last for a very long time.

Find some friends. Find a good source of caffeine and a TV show that makes you laugh. Take naps when you can or go for a run if you're one of those weirdos who love that. Eat dark chocolate late at night. (Have another piece in the morning if you need it.)

Hang in there, friends. You're going to go the distance.

9

You Can't Treat Me Like This. I Am Not A Stick![1]

After the fiery tempest that was my oldest daughter, my son felt like an easy child. Scott was a great sleeper. He could play by himself for hours. He was highly emotional, but he didn't aim his emotions at me as a weapon.

Essentially, when he was little and able to live in his own private world, things were smooth sailing. As he got older, though, his quick mind developed much faster than his body. He had thoughts, opinions, and very definite expectations that the world did not always live up to. He got frustrated. He wanted control, but, you know, no one gives much control to a five-year-old.

---

[1] This is a direct quote from Scott one night when he had been sent to his room for some infraction. Apparently, a stick is the most worthless thing he could think of, and he would not be regarded as such.

In those years from five to ten, we went head to head on a regular basis. He didn't lose his mind like his sister had; he was just so very sure that he was *right*. Even when he was completely wrong.[2]

By this point, I had learned with Ellie to drop arguments when they got heated, send her somewhere to cool off, and resume the conversation when she had regained the ability to think rationally. With Scott, I quickly discovered that I needed a different tactic. Dropping a subject just left him sure that he was right, and when I picked it back up again later, he was even more angry that I was revisiting a battle he felt he'd already won. Which meant there was no giving in. I had to stay in it with him and bring my best-crafted arguments until he admitted defeat. Though please note that defeat didn't ever look like him admitting I was right. It was just the point when he stopped arguing back because his logic failed before mine.

I was born for this kind of conflict.

Let me be clear: these arguments were never about whether or not he would obey me. In our house, if I say you're taking a bath, you're taking a bath. Refusing is not an option. But my kids are smart and strong-willed, and I

---

[2] For example, at various points he was certain that there was no point in bathing daily, that haircuts were for losers, that his sisters should be punished severely for taking his seat on the couch, and that letting his dad eat the last brownie when I had refused to let him do the same was a clear injustice.

like that about them. So if they want to debate the merits of bathing, I'll go five rounds. Because I want more than just their obedience in bathing tonight. I want them to understand the reasons why bathing is important, to believe in the cause of cleanliness, so that one day they can stand on their own two sweet-smelling feet.

On a few memorable occasions, though, Scott would not admit defeat.

When he was about eight, we had an epic face-off. Like so many of these things, it sounds ridiculous, but here's how it went down:

After dinner one night, Nate and Scott were in the front room while I put a few items of food away. I called in to Scott and asked him to do some small chore.

Under his breath, but still very audible, he said something to the effect of, "Ugh, I have to do everything."

"Excuse me?" I said. "Don't even start with me. You have to do everything? How many things do I do for you? How many things does your dad do?"

"What?" he wailed, tears in his eyes. "Why are you yelling at me?" (Note: I was lecturing, not yelling.)

"Because you just said that you have to do everything!"

"No, I didn't! I never said that!"

Now I was mad. Stand by your words or don't stand by your words, kid, but don't try to rewrite the history of the last five minutes.

"You did say that. You can't deny something that I just heard with my own two ears and pretend it didn't happen."

"No, I didn't!"

"Then what did you say?"

"I didn't say anything!"

At this point, Nate got involved. "You did, son. I heard you, too."

"I didn't!"

"Now you're lying! You need to apologize to your mother."

Cue wounded tears at this horribly unfounded accusation and a total absence of any kind of admission or apology.

Long story short, he was sent to his room to stay up there until he was willing to admit the truth and apologize. He would miss out on the family show we were watching downstairs. He would miss out on dessert. He would stay there until he was ready to be honest.

He said he'd stay there forever.

We went downstairs to watch TV with the girls. I was miserable, as I always am when there's unhappiness in the house, but I also knew that this was necessary. I could hear some thumping upstairs. I knew Scott was furious at the perceived injustice. I told myself to let it be.

An hour or so later, I went up to see if he was ready to apologize. He was sitting on his bed, stony-faced. He still didn't see why we were handing out such a huge consequence for something that never happened. (You guys, it happened. But how do you debate reality with someone?)[3] He cried, but they were angry tears, not repentant ones. Discouraged, feeling the nagging anxiety that I was raising someone with sociopathic tendencies, I went back downstairs.

I happened to glance out the window, and I saw a blue and white blanket on the back lawn.

At first I didn't think much of it. Maybe you don't have the kind of kids who take all manner of household objects outside to play and then casually leave them there to be destroyed by the elements, but I definitely do. Still, this was Scott's every-night sleeping blanket, so I was irritated that he would leave it there.

I went out to pick it up, which is when I noticed the slightly askew screen on the second floor. The location of

---

[3] This is not a political statement, 2020 aside. It's the historic cry of every parent with a stubborn child.

the blanket suddenly seemed significant. It was right under Scott's window.

I went back upstairs. The boy was still lying on his bed, face set and angry.

"Did you throw this out the window?" I held up his beloved snuggly blanket.

I could tell for a minute he wanted to deny it, but then he gritted his teeth and said, "Yes."

"Did you take your screen off to throw it out?"

"Yes."

"Why?"

There was a pause, but he wasn't considering a lie this time. He wanted to tell me.

"I was going to jump out and leave, but after I threw the blanket out, I decided not to."

You guys. That boy is terrified of heights. When he was one year old, his big sister convinced him to climb up a fully enclosed plastic structure at a playground. Halfway up, he froze, so incapacitated by fear that it took Nate half an hour to talk him down.

But on this night, he was so angry at his unjust incarceration that he actively considered jumping from a second story window to escape it.

He stayed in his room the rest of the night. At bedtime, Nate went in to talk to him. I'd like to say that Scott admitted defeat and apologized. I'd like to say that we won him over with our firm discipline. But I don't think that's what happened. I don't know exactly how the conversation went, but I do know that some kind of small acknowledgment was made and that we all moved on the next day.

Anger fades. Disagreements are put behind us.

But some things are not forgotten. A few months ago, that night got mentioned again. It was Scott who brought it up. That was one of the only times he was "grounded," and he's still bitter about it. He's still convinced that he had done nothing wrong and was unjustly punished.

What can I say? Sometimes your kids just think you are wrong. Sometimes they don't ever come around to your point of view.

Worse, sometimes I *am* wrong. I made my son mad this very morning by making a decision he disagreed with. And in retrospect, his understanding of the situation was more accurate than mine, so I get why it irritated him.

Luckily, we will be okay. Anger fades. Disagreements are put behind us.

Bearing with each other and forgiving each other are the key to any relationship, so why should the parent/child relationship be any different?

Sometimes we make each other mad. Sometimes we disagree, and there isn't a path to seeing eye to eye. Learning that we can live with that, that we can love each other and be close to one another *even while we're angry* is one of the most beautiful lessons my adult life has taught me.

I can think you're wrong and still think you're wonderful.

I can argue heatedly with you today and still laugh with you tomorrow.

I can be furious with you and still never leave you.

That's love.

That's the love God's given to me and the love that I give to my children. And wondrously, miraculously, that's the love they are learning to give to me.

I'll take it over winning every argument any day.

10

Kids Are Tougher, And Weirder, Than You Think

Once I saw a series of posters made by a dad, each one an illustration of something he had said to his kids that he never imagined having to say. They included things like "I'm not talking to you until you're wearing underwear," and "No, the leprechaun is staying in my pocket," but my favorite one of all was the most basic: "Don't lick my arm. That's what weird kids do."[1]

"That's what weird kids do," is the subtext of many of my lessons on manners.

In the checkout line: "Don't kiss the railing! I don't care if it's shiny." At the breakfast table: "Don't take off your shirt! One drop of milk won't kill you." On the couch: "No, you can't explore my ear with your toe!" At bedtime: "No,

---

[1] Nathan Ripperger has an Etsy shop (https://etsy.me/1bvPoz6) but the last time I checked, he didn't have anything for sale.

you can't sleep in the clothes you plan to wear tomorrow to save time."

My kids have a never-ending supply of ways to be weird.

Scott was a particularly quirky and imaginative little buddy. From his earliest days, he personified everything in his life. He would take the caps off of markers and stick them on the ends of his fingers, making each one into a character. Then Mr. Blue and Mrs. Red and Mr. Green would have conversations. Strapped in a booster seat at a restaurant, he'd lay out the sugar packets and they would have adventures with the sweeteners. At home in his highchair with nothing in reach, he'd use his hands. ("Hello, hand!" "Hello, other hand! How are you today?")

Bedtime was prime time for him. Unlike his older sister, he loved that half hour between being put in his crib and falling asleep. We could tell he was using it to process his day because we would hear him repeating new words he had learned over and over or, when he was a bit older, quoting conversations we'd had or saying people's names and laughing to himself.[2]

When he was five, we moved home from Argentina, and for the first time, he had his own room while the girls

---

[2] Okay, so it was a little creepy sometimes. He had this gravelly voice, so when he muttered, "Felipe" and then imitated Felipe's laugh, it gave you pause.

shared. He loved that room, playing Legos in it and trying out experiments.[3] He had a big double bed, and snuggling in was his favorite thing.

And then one day I came to tuck him in, and he was on the floor. He had put his pillow and blankets right next to his bed instead of on it. He seemed happy, and it wasn't hurting anything, so I didn't object. I just knelt down, gave him a hug and a kiss, and said goodnight.

The next night, he was in the same spot, right in that little strip of carpet between the bed and the door. I asked why he was sleeping on the floor. He said he just wanted to. Okay, then.

The next night was the same. And then the next. I would wake up each morning and he'd be framed in the doorway, fast asleep on the floor. After a week, I asked again if he wouldn't be more comfortable in his bed. He said no.

A few weeks went by. We bought a new house. As we prepared to move into it, I had long talks with him about his room. I asked a lot of questions and tried to arrange everything so he'd be comfortable to sleep in his own bed again. He said he might. We moved. He slept on the floor of his new room.

---

[3] Like the one where he put a pillow on his lamp to make cool shadows. It only caught on fire a little bit.

As those first couple of weeks passed, his sleeping spot crept closer to the door, then into the doorway, and finally into the hall. Every few days I would ask a question or two. Was there something in his room he was afraid of? Did he feel lonely in there? Was his bed uncomfortable? No and no and no. He just liked sleeping here. And every few weeks, Nate and I would talk. Should we keep allowing this? Was there something we should do? Every time, we decided to just let it run its course.

That boy slept on the floor in the hallway for a year.

Then one day when he was approaching seven years old, he told me about one small change I could make to his room. When we moved in, we had removed his broken closet doors, and he wanted me to put them back on.

"If I do that, will you sleep in your own bed?" I asked.

"Maybe."

I reinstalled the closet doors. He moved back into his room. He's been sleeping in bed like a normal person ever since.[4]

Who even knows what's going on in their little heads? Every time I think I understand how weird my kids can be, they have found a new way to surprise me. And they are not alone. All the best kids I know are little weirdos.

---

[4] I've asked, but to this day he never has explained to me what was going on that year.

A few things I have known real children to do: Refuse to walk on shiny polished floors because they looked like a hole in the earth. Spend hours crawling around collecting leaves and sticks, pretending to be a "medicine cat."[5] Talk to an imaginary friend at the dinner table instead of to the real humans sitting there. Make up stories about animals dying violent deaths. Refuse to wear any pants that don't have an elastic waist. Write poems about the people they love persecuting them. Sing their responses to every question. Stick a dime up their nose just to see if it would fit. Find a way to introduce the feelings of their cat into every conversation.

I could tell you those things only happened when they were little, but I'd be lying. Most of them aren't outgrowing the weirdness.

And why should they? If normal means "average," why would that be our goal? In our house, the word "weird" is not an insult. We've been affectionately calling our children "little weirdos" as long as they've been alive, and they wear it like a badge of honor.

That's not to say that weirdness doesn't come with risks. The reason people learn to blend into the pack is that being wildly different draws all kinds of negative

---

[5] If you've read the *Warriors* books, you get it. If not, imagine secret clans of cats who look down on house pets and read prophecies in the stars. In other words, books designed by weirdos for weirdos. They are delightful.

attention. Weirdness invites mockery, it can lead to isolation, and it can distract people from the awesomeness that goes with it.

To some degree, it's our job as parents to teach our kids how to fit in. We are the ones responsible for helping them navigate the world. In the real world, wearing a superhero costume every day is adorable when you're five, but when you're twenty-five, it will get in the way of your life goals. You don't actually get to act however you want in life. Not if you want a career. Or a spouse. Or friends. Someone needs to tell you this before it's too late.

I was lucky enough to have a mom who helped me with that. When I was seven, I developed the habit of yawning wide every few minutes because I felt an uncontrollable urge to stretch out the corners of my mouth. Where did this little bit of weirdness come from? I have no idea, but I remember how necessary it felt at the time. And I remember the look my mom gave me when she saw me do it. It took her weeks of constant reminders to break me of the habit.

But I also remember that while my mom helped me realize how bizarre my behavior looked to other people, she never acted like there was anything wrong with me. I'll always be thankful for that.

Because all the weird things going on in my mind, the things that led me to act strangely and also be completely unaware of my eccentricity, were also the building blocks of my creative ability to solve problems and ask questions and tell stories. It would have been easy to overlook that. The world would try to make me ashamed of how my mind worked, but my parents, though they didn't always understand it, let me know they thought my mind was something wonderful. It made all the difference.

So yes, I have taught my kids not to put their feet on people. Or talk loudly about strangers. Or sleep in their next-day clothes. Because I want them to know that some behaviors will be off-putting to others. But I do let them pick out their own outfits and hairstyles. I encourage them to read their oddball novels and hang geeky posters on their walls. I egg on their curiosity and enthusiasm and don't laugh when they use big words that make them sound like fifty-year-old professors. I let them sleep on the floor if they want to.

I know other people do laugh at them sometimes. I know people roll their eyes. I know the world isn't always kind to my little weirdos. Obviously, I hate that, but I really don't worry about it too much.

Because kids aren't just weirder than we expect, they are also tougher than we give them credit for.

When the older kids were seven and five, we enrolled them in Little League. Nate is a huge baseball fan, and one of the things he was most excited about in being back in the US was the chance for the kids to play ball.

I was thrilled for Ellie to start. That girl was born to play a team sport, and a half season of field hockey in

Argentina had proved that her options there weren't the best fit. I knew she would take to softball right away. But Scott, my sensitive little weirdo, had me concerned. Up to that point, he had shown no interest in sports. He loved to play alone, and even when we were with his best friends, he'd often go off by himself. He was terrified of heights and cautious around water, so I wasn't sure what other fears might surface. And he regularly cried at any and every frustration. How was he going to handle learning a difficult physical skill?

I took him to his first t-ball practice fully prepared to have him running to me in tears before it was half over.

I could have saved myself the worry. My little guy didn't have any ball skills at that first practice, and he was (and is) the slowest runner out there. But he stood in the field as the coach gave simple instructions, and his face was set with determination. That whole season, while other kids wandered the outfield or sat down to pick flowers, Scott was focused on the ball. He learned the rules. He learned the skills. He's been playing baseball ever since.

I can't tell you how many times, over the years, I've watched my son well up with tears on the ball field. He wears his heart on his sleeve, and baseball can be a very frustrating sport. But I also watch him hold in those tears. I watch him bring himself under control. I watch him play on, even when his face is red or he can't help muttering under his breath. Baseball is something he loves, and he knows it takes self-control to get better.

A couple years back, he joined the Cross-Country team just to stay in shape during baseball's off season. He hated it. The coach was intense, and Scott is not a runner. Several times he threw up at practice, and for the first month, he held back tears nearly every time I dropped him off. Nate and I agreed that if he asked to quit, we'd let him. I expected to have the conversation at any moment, and honestly a part of me hoped it would happen. I hated seeing him so miserable. But he never asked. He not only stuck it out through the season but he returned to run the next year and the next. He bonded with the coach and the other runners, and the experience has been amazing for him.

I have been guilty of underestimating my kids' toughness over and over again. I know them so well. I am privy to their weakest moments. The mama-bear urge to protect them, even from themselves, overwhelms me sometimes.

But God made us to do hard things. He made my kids to do hard things. Who am I to hold them back?

So I let them take risks and be passionate and weird. Because I trust that the God who made them knows what he is doing.

I trust that my kids can be mocked and still maintain the self-confidence we have instilled in them. That they can have their ideas shot down and be resourceful enough to come up with creative solutions. That they can be misunderstood and learn how to communicate more effectively. That they can even lose friends sometimes and still have the courage to find new ones.

I trust that they can use their weirdness to find new strength and their strength to make room for more weirdness.

And the world will be a better place because those tough little weirdos are in it.

11

I Asked For A Day With No Whining And All I Got Was This Stupid T-shirt

My husband thinks I'm awesome. Really. He tells me so all the time, and though I'm fairly certain he's delusional, I shamelessly encourage this kind of talk. It doesn't even matter if it's true; it's just great to hear my favorite person say that my accomplishments are significant and my flaws adorable. I need that kind of encouragement.

Because my kids are a whole different story and there are three of them, you know?

My kids love me and are attached to me, for sure, but they are also 100 percent dedicated to communicating their honest evaluation of my work as a mom. And frankly, they have concerns.

They've always been this way. I don't just mean the crying anytime they need something or the casual refusal to eat carefully prepared foods. I mean, they have very particular opinions about my skills and life choices.

I can still remember sitting on Ellie's bed when she was just a toddler. We had finished reading her nightly books and I was ready to sing her a song before she went to sleep. I started something simple and sweet, and her face got dark. Before two words were out of my mouth, she reached her hand up and covered my mouth. "No," she said.

That was her final word on the matter. From that day on, anytime I tried to sing to my child, she would immediately shut me down, often by physically blocking my mouth. Please understand that singing was an important part of my life. I'm no Mariah Carey, but I wasn't warbling off tune, either. For whatever unknowable reason, though, Ellie just didn't want to hear it.

And so a sweetly-imagined scene of motherhood bit the dust.

In my kids' eyes, I fell short in so many ways. When Scott was two, we got a Wii, and occasionally I'd unwind in the evening by playing some Super Mario Bros. It was so far removed from any of my normal activities that it was the perfect escape, and if the kids were around, they'd be entertained for quite a while by Mario's antics on the screen. I thought I was really onto something the night that Scott watched with rapt attention for a good half hour.

Then he stood up.

"Papi is a lot better at this than you," he said as he walked away. He never spent much time watching me after that.[1]

I can't tell you the number of birthdays or Mother's Days that I thought, "It's my special day. Maybe my kids will treat me special today," only to have them complain about dinner and argue when I asked to take a family picture just like it was any other day. More than once I told them that the only present I wanted was a day with no whining. Instead I got Barbie hair clips and a Batman t-shirt along with the normal dose of disapproval.

The main piece of advice Nate gives to new dads is to tell their wives early and often how wonderful they are. "Kids mainly give negative feedback," he tells them. "She doesn't need you to criticize. She already feels like a failure. She needs you to tell her that she's doing a great job."

I'm Deb Dunlevy, and I approved this message.

As my kids have gotten older, they've picked up on their dad's attitude, and now they sometimes show approval

---

[1] Some things really do not change over time. After years of having no time for video games, I recently started playing on the Nintendo during the Covid-19 quarantine. Scott and Ellie spent hours watching me play for the sole purpose of laughing at how bad I am. They would shout instructions through their roars of laughter. And truthfully, as long as I completely debased my pride, it was a pretty fun bonding experience.

mixed in with their disdain. I appreciate these moments of affirmation, but I've learned not to count on them. Kids are wonderful for many things, but you can't let their opinion of you matter too much. Mostly because if you do, you'll be deeply disappointed when you realize that they aren't thinking about you at all.

Like many moms, I have one of those memory apps on my phone, the ones that show whatever you posted on social media on that day in previous years. I know it's one of the most mom-ish things I do, but I seriously check it every day. It's not so much that I'm sentimental.[2] I just love feeling like my past life experiences are here with me today. It gives me perspective. It makes life feel integrated.

And some days it makes me laugh until tears run down my face.

It's full of examples of how little consideration my kids are giving to the rest of my life. A few weeks ago I came across this amazing tweet from 2014. For a few days, I had been tracking the memories of my excitement leading up to the publishing of my third book, *The Secret Source*. The cover had been designed. The formatting was in place. Finally, a year's worth of work was coming to fruition. Then this:

---

[2] I'm more of a long-for-the-future than a long-for-the-past kind of girl.

Just told my son I ordered the proof of my NEW BOOK. He shrugged and shuffled off because no one is as unimpressed by you as your children.

Oh, Lord, were truer words ever spoken?

Last fall, when my novel *TWIN* came out, I had a book launch event at a local bookstore. Like most authors, I don't love the publicity part of my job, but I was excited about this book and thrilled that it was finally out in the world. I had worked for weeks preparing everything, had promoted the event, had chosen an outfit with my daughters' help, and on launch day I was high on adrenaline.

I arrived before my family to set up and get ready. Things were looking good by the time they got there, and the kids rushed in to see me. Lucy gave me a silent hug, and Scott grabbed my arm.

"Mom," he said. "I just remembered I have to have my whole science fair experiment done by Monday morning, so we need to do it today!"

Right. Of course. Let me just press pause on my important professional day and try to think about the boiling points of salt water.

The event went great. Enough people showed up to fill the bookstore space, my reading was well-received, and we sold a bunch of books. I chatted with friends and strangers about books and writing. I signed copies of my published works. When I finally wrapped everything up, loaded the book boxes back in the car, and drove home, I was exhausted but happy.

I walked in the door, desperate for dinner and caffeine, and Scott met me just inside.

"I have the ingredients all laid out. Whenever you're ready, we can start the experiment."

And just like that, the day was no longer about me. I took off my boots and my dangly earrings and turned back into Just Plain Mom.

Ego has no place in parenting. Like, literally, there just isn't room for it.

If you've ever come home from the job where you were absolutely killing it only to be greeted by non-stop complaints about dinner, you're a parent.

If you've ever sat down from a public speaking engagement to find a text on your phone that someone threw up, you're a parent.

If you've ever received an important award and then spent the car ride home listening to the woes of sixth grade homework, you're a parent.

I've never met Beyoncé or her undoubtedly beautiful babies, but I am confident that even her children are not impressed by her. Never mind that she's beautiful, famous, and fabulously wealthy. Never mind that she's one of the most talented people on the planet. Kids don't give a crap about any of that. I'm not saying that they don't receive the benefits of her success. I'm not saying that they won't be proud of her as they grow up. But they will not be impressed. To them, she'll be Just Plain Mom.

I think about this from time to time, when I feel deflated by the lack of admiration from my kids. I think how lucky I am to have them, these little people who see me every morning when I first wake up, who have watched me cut up their sandwiches and clean up their messes, who have witnessed all my flaws up close. In a me-centered world, it's an incredible blessing to have sweet innocents who will poke holes in your pride whether you need it or not.

They aren't here for my accomplishments. They're here for my love.

It's not terribly uplifting, but it's a real gift. My accomplishments will come and go. My success will be fleeting if it comes at all. But my kids' love for me isn't based on anything other than my existence in their world. All they want from me is me.

And, you know, some help with this dang science fair experiment.

12

If It's Good Enough for The Dog, It Probably Won't Kill The Kid

Of the hundreds of scientific and theological questions my kids have asked me over the years, there is one I dread more than any other.

"How much more do I need to eat?"

Really. This question has been posed to me at least two to three times a week for the last fourteen years, and it stumps me every time.

It always starts the same way: "Mom, I'm done."

I look at the plate. Only three bites have been taken and none of them contained color. Clearly, the child needs to eat more than three mouthfuls of mashed potatoes.

"No," I say. "You aren't done. You need to eat some of your chicken and your peas."

I'm on fairly solid ground here. If asked my reasoning, it would be that children need protein and vegetables to be healthy and that they have currently eaten none.

But then the dreaded question. "How much do I need to eat?"

True answer: I have no earthly idea how much the child should eat. I am not a nutritionist. I am not a doctor. I have no special knowledge of child development, and I haven't been keeping track of their caloric intake for the day.

Answer I give: Three bites of each.

Sometimes it's five. Or seven.

It. Is. Totally. Random.

Why did no one warn me before I became a parent about how many daily decisions I would have to make with no discernible reasoning behind them?

I've tried inventing reasoning, but if I'm being honest, my "reasons" are sometimes really weak. At some point along the way, I gave myself permission to admit that the basis for these decisions is simple: I do what I can live with. Will I feel guilty if they eat no vegetables at all? Then I make them eat some. Does it sound exhausting to sit there for twenty minutes just to force them to eat four bites? Then three bites is probably enough!

Because I'm a person who loves consistent logic and objective principles, for a long time I resisted the idea that it might be okay for us all to just do what works for us. But it was living overseas, raising kids in the middle of two cultural systems, that really pushed me over the edge.

When Ellie was a toddler, she was obsessed with club crackers. You know those pale rectangles with the crumbly edges and the buttery taste? They were available everywhere in our neighborhood, and they were a staple in our house. She loved them so much that the word *tita*, short for *galletita*, was one of her first ten words and probably the very first that she learned in Spanish.[1]

Like all toddlers, though, Ellie had a short attention span, and she developed a habit of asking for a cracker, taking one bite, then dropping the cracker on the floor only to ask for another a few minutes later. At first, I didn't notice and would be amazed at how many crackers she ate, until later in the day when I discovered fourteen half-eaten crackers collecting ants in the corner. I started keeping better track, and when she dropped them, I would pick them up for her and give them back the next time she asked for one. Unfortunately, she didn't want a cracker that already had a bite out of it. She wanted a whole cracker, and she was suspicious of these half-

---

[1] She discovered early on in life that it paid to ask for cookies or crackers in Spanish because Argentines will never, ever say no to a child. Especially an adorably sassy blonde child.

eaten ones. WHY WAS I TAKING BITES OUT OF HER CRACKERS?

So, I developed a rule. If she dropped a cracker, the next time she wanted one, she had to pick up the one she'd dropped and eat it first. Then and only then could she have more.

This all made perfect sense to me, training my child not to be wasteful and not to make unnecessary messes. Plus, let's be honest, it saved my pregnant self from bending over more than I already had to.

Then one day we went to visit a lady in the neighborhood. I'd been working hard to build a friendship with her, and she loved Ellie to pieces. As always when I took Ellie along to what I hoped would be an adult conversation, I brought snacks and a couple of toys. So, there I was, chatting happily with this nice neighbor when Ellie dropped her cracker on the floor. Not two seconds later, she asked for another and I told her to eat that one first.

You should have seen the look of horror on my neighbor's face.

I will acknowledge a few key points which must have loomed large in this lady's mind. One, the floor was rough-poured cement and admittedly not the cleanest. Two, I was refusing to give a cracker to a child even though I had a whole box of crackers RIGHT THERE. Three, the floor was where animals ate, not adorable children.

It was like I was some kind of monster. My neighbor did the whole oh-mama-just-let-the-sweet-thing-have-a-teeny-weeny-cracker thing. I explained our issue and what I was trying to teach her. I might as well have been that adult voice from the Peanuts cartoon. "Wah-wah-wah-wah-wah."

By this time, Ellie had sensed her opportunity and was loudly refusing to pick up the cracker from the floor while continuing to beg for a new one. Armed with the stubbornness of my German foremothers, I was determined not to cave because I didn't want to reward her continued defiance.

Of course, my neighbor quickly cut the Gordian knot by pulling out a bag of iced cookies and offering Ellie as many as she would like. I had no choice but to sit there and be pleasant while my daughter ate cookies. That and meekly pick the cracker up off the floor before we left.

And this round goes to the cute toddler.

So incredibly annoying, right? If I had been allowed to continue the cracker standoff indefinitely, I would have eventually won, my daughter would have submitted obediently, and she would not have grown up to be the horrible entitled monster that she is today.

Wait...

What I mean is that if I had just learned the lesson that my neighbor was trying to teach me, if I had stopped after that day and not made my daughter eat crackers from dirty floors for the next two weeks, then my daughter wouldn't have been shamed, wouldn't have ingested so much dirt, and wouldn't have grown up to be the sickly, insecure waif she is today.

Wait...

As far as I can tell, the outcome of the great cracker standoff of 2006 didn't have any impact on my daughter's ultimate development at all.

I think the thing that is so hard about being a mom[2] is that you put in so much effort to make the right decisions for your kids every day and then it turns out that really, they were going to be fine either way.

I mean, there are outer boundaries to this, of course. I still think giving kids what they want every time they throw a fit is a pretty sure way to raise bratty humans. And I know for sure that abuse of any kind leaves scars that linger for life. It's definitely not okay to starve your kids or to abandon them. It's definitely important to teach them the basics of life like how to use a toilet and how to read.

But whether you let your kids drink fruit punch from a sippy cup or give them nothing but organic milk until they're twelve, honestly, it's all good. Whether you have an elaborate bedtime routine or just send them upstairs

---

[2] Right, like there is just this one thing.

with a kiss and a good-night is your call. Whether you potty train them at eighteen months with a well-regulated method or slowly wean them off pull ups when they're five, whether you send them off to school to learn their letters or teach them at home or do some combination of both, it's all about what works for you.

In the US, I know parents who sleep trained their babies at four months old. In Argentina, I knew mothers who spent an hour rocking their child to sleep each night until the kid was five. As far as I can tell, the kids raised both ways have grown up with an equal chance of being well-adjusted adults.

When Ellie was an infant, I worried constantly about how I was going to be responsible to make sure this child ate three healthy meals a day FOR EIGHTEEN YEARS. I nursed her exclusively for five months, and then I knew it was time to start the process of actually making choices about food. My stress level about the transition was through the roof.

I wrote to my sister-in-law, who had babies a little before me, begging for her help. She sent a chart she had used, laying out how to introduce foods one at a time and which ones should be introduced at which age. It even listed amounts per day. It was, as the Argentines would say, the most "Yanqui" thing ever.[3] I loved it.

---

[3] "Yanqui" as in "Yankee" as in "North American" as in "white people, man."

I also sought advice from my Argentine pediatrician. Through a friend, we had found a wonderful old doctor who ran a private practice out of a tiny house not far from us. We had already seen him once or twice, and we smiled through every visit.

He was a short man with delicate white hair and a gentle, soothing voice. When he examined the baby, he would talk through what he was doing in a sing-song pattern, saying the same things at every visit. "Tiene la nariz limpia...tiene la panza blandita..." The nose is clean...the belly is soft...

At Ellie's five-month checkup, after the exam, the doctor mentioned that it was about time to start the baby on solid foods. He said he would give me a list of foods he recommended we begin with, and then he sat down and began writing on his little prescription pad. When he finished, he handed it to me, a short list in swooping cursive that matched his voice and personality.

Translated into English, here is what it said:

Baby Cereal

Jell-O

Soft fruits

Sprite (left out to go flat)

Yogurt

Soft cooked eggs

I stared at the piece of paper. He asked if I had any questions. I looked at the top where his name and medical degree were printed. I had many questions, but I said I didn't. I folded up the paper and put it in my purse.

In the car, Nate and I looked at the list together. It was like an artifact from a far-off time.

"Why would you give a baby flat Sprite?" Nate asked.

"Why would you give a baby Jell-O?" I responded.

"Because Jell-O is good," he said.

We laughed all the way home where I put the list of foods recommended by a medical professional next to my sister-in-law's detailed chart. It was a study in cultural differences.

When the time came to feed my baby, I went with the chart. What can I say? I'm North American, and scientific charts make more sense to me.

But I kept that hand-written list nearby, not because I wanted an excuse to give my baby Jell-O but because I wanted to remember that there are lots of ways to feed a child. That doctor had been giving nutritional advice to Argentine mothers for decades, and their children had grown up healthy. They had turned into functional adults. Many of them brought their own children back to the same sweet man who had treated them.

There are way fewer absolutes about child-raising than the internet would have you believe. So much of what we do is governed by the instincts that we inherited from our culture. And then there are the things we do just because they suit us as individuals.

Several years ago, Nate started calling the sum of the small everyday choices we make our *parenting aesthetic*. I have found it to be such a useful concept. It's not about right or wrong. It's not about what's good for your kids or bad for them. It's about what you like, how you want to live, and what you can survive for eighteen years to life. It's about where you land on the giant spectrum that covers everything that isn't evil.

In our house, we don't allow screaming. This is because I have sensitive ears and can't stand shrill noises. We do allow the strong and forceful expression of emotions (sometimes known as yelling or sassing). This is because Nate and I are both passionate people who accept aggression well and prefer to have things out in the open.

In our house, we don't ever call each other stupid but are very comfortable calling each other weird.

In our house, we watch tons of television and analyze our favorite shows on a regular basis. We derive a great deal of joy from our mutual love of fictional characters.

In our house, we don't do puzzles. We just don't like them. We encourage board games but don't play them with our kids very often because we find playing board games with our kids irritating.

In our house, we live with two animals because we like animals. Our kids have to take care of their pets every day.

In our house, I pack the kids' lunches. They have more household chores in the summer and very few during the school year. Why? Because that's what works for me.

Not a single one of those choices is the way things "should" be done. It's just the way Nate and I want to live. And so we do.

We have friends who allow, and even encourage, their kids to shout and be loud indoors. It doesn't bother them, and they want their kids to be free. Cool.

We have friends who strictly limit screen time for their kids and go for long runs as a family, in all weather. That's the kind of life they enjoy and feel healthiest living. Cool.

We have friends who play games every Friday night with their kids and even invite other kids to join in. Cool.

We have friends whose kids pack their own lunches and clean the whole house every weekend. Cool.

You know what all those people have in common? They've been parenting for years, and they're still sane.[4]

---

[4] Mostly.

And they're all pretty happy, too. Why? Because they're choosing what they can live with and owning the choices they make. Their parenting aesthetic is different from ours, but that doesn't make it worse (or better).

And yeah, sometimes we have to make allowances for each other and work a little harder than we'd like to live with each other's parenting aesthetic. But if our kids are weirder than we thought, why shouldn't our friends be? And if our kids are tougher than we thought, why can't we be?

So set any bedtime you want and pick a number of bites out of thin air.

You do what you have to do, and I'll do what I can live with. And we'll all try to stay sane together.

13

There IS Such A Thing As TMI, Karen

We don't go in for potty humor at our house. It's an aesthetic thing. It's not about judging anyone. We just don't think it's funny.

That's why I hesitated to write this chapter. First of all, this is some serious TMI. Secondly, though I don't deny that it's funny, it's just not my favorite way to laugh.

But I promised myself I'd be real, and well, this is as real as it gets.

When Scott was in Kindergarten, his school had a special Mother/Son Game Night.[1] I think the idea was to counterbalance that they were one of the only public schools still throwing a Father/Daughter Dance every winter. Whatever the reason, Scott loved the sound of "game night," so we went.

---

[1] Yes, I am deeply aware that this sounds a lot like *Arrested Development's* "Motherboy." I swore to Nate if I saw anyone in matching costumes, I'd turn around and come straight home.

They had a pretty cute setup. When we walked in the door, there was a little photo booth to please the moms, and then they gave us each a score sheet and pencil. The idea was to walk around the school, visiting different game stations, and pitting mother versus son at each game. We were to keep track of how many wins we had, and when we arrived at the end, there would be cookies and prizes. Scott was thrilled.

We had a great time together. I won the ring toss and the hallway bowling. He won the memory game and the pull-up competition. We paused for some fruit punch, and then I took him in one-on-one basketball (he was six). When we came to the jump rope station, he was determined not to go down.

They handed us each one of those school jump ropes with the plastic beads and sent us out onto the gym floor. It was a straight up counting game; the person with the most jumps before they got tangled up or tired out was the winner. I hadn't jumped rope in years, but it was a favorite pastime as a kid, so I knew I could give Scott a run for his money. A teacher blew the whistle. We began to jump at the same time.

And then I made a horrible discovery. Since the last time I had jumped rope, not only had I gotten twenty years older, I had carried three babies to full term, the last one just a few years prior. I had thought my body was fully recovered from Lucy's birth, had lost the baby weight, had gotten in decent shape. But I had never intentionally drunk a full cup of fruit punch and then jumped up and down repeatedly. Turned out, my bladder control wasn't quite up to the challenge.

For the first four or five jumps, I was fine. Then I began to feel a tiny bit of pee each time I landed. There was no sudden rush, but after a few more jumps, I could tell the cumulative effect was going to be a problem. My little son was looking at me with his hyper-focused competitive gaze. He was jumping steadily. I did the only decent thing I could do. I faked a stumble, conceded the win, and as gracefully as possible excused myself to the restroom where I discovered that I had, in fact, noticeably peed my pants.

It was one of those nightmare scenarios from childhood which theoretically should be so much better when you're an adult. Yes, a truly embarrassing thing had happened right there at school in front of everyone, but now I had keys to my very own car and could slip out the back door and go home without anyone being the wiser.

Here's the dilemma, though. My son still had no idea that anything had happened. And he was having a great time. We had a set of table games and then the award ceremony to get through before the event ended, and there was no way to leave early without disappointing Scott and probably also having to admit what happened.

So, I didn't. Instead, I took off my sweater, tied it strategically around my waist, and headed back to play Connect Four with my son, careful to keep my purse in maximum blockage position.

I was deeply uncomfortable, in both mind and body. I was also competitively compromised, so my son ended up winning the overall competition. Losing would normally have rankled, but when I realized they were making all the winners line up along the front to receive their awards, I was happy not to join them. I sat at a table in the corner, nibbling a cookie my son had brought me and waited out the speeches and announcements.

But when we finally made it home and into dry clothes at the end of the night, my son was still blissfully ignorant of my plight. So you tell me who really won.

We're all about honesty and openness in this family. We never told our kids Santa was real, and we barely acknowledged the Tooth Fairy at all. My kids know I have chocolate that I sometimes eat even after I've told them they can't have dessert. We talk openly about the hard stuff of life and when global tragedy strikes, we discuss it without sugarcoating. We admit to our kids that there are things we don't know and we apologize when we are in the wrong.

All that honesty doesn't mean we tell our kids everything, though. We aren't trying to be superheroes, but we ARE adults. We don't need to burden our kids with our burdens. We don't expect our kids to be our support system. They're not here to meet our emotional needs—that's what we have friends and adult family members for.

There have been times, when I was exhausted and stressed out and my kids were relentless with their needs and complaints, that I have wished they could understand what it feels like to be me. It would be so nice to be fully appreciated and to have my state of mind considered in their choices. But when I'm rational, I'm glad they don't know about the stress of grownup life and the weird little sacrifices I make for them.

Because even when it's funny, adult life is messy and hard. They'll have to face all that eventually, but I can give them a few more years of blessed ignorance. There are some things they just aren't ready to know.

For example, no kid needs to know that pregnancy wrecked his mother's body in ways he would never be able to imagine. And no kid ever needs to know that his mom peed her pants.

Which I guess means I can never let my kids read this chapter.

Probably just as well.

14

What? This Fist Doesn't Mean I'm Going To Punch You.

When we moved an hour south of Buenos Aires to the city of La Plata, one of the things we were most excited about was the zoo. La Plata had a city zoo that was easy to get to, practically free, and filled with playgrounds and shady picnic spots alongside the somewhat raggedy collection of animals.

Ellie was four, Scott was two, I was three months pregnant, and it was summer. We went to the zoo often.

One weekend we had guests staying with us, so we decided to go show them our favorite spot. It was a lovely December day, not too hot, not too cold. We pushed Scott in the stroller while Ellie capered about like the little mountain goat she was. We had made the big circle of the park and were coming back toward the front gate when we stopped for a few minutes by the sea lion exhibit. It was an outdoor lake of sorts with a shoulder-high stone wall around it. Since shoulder-high to an adult is too-tall-to-see for a child, they had conveniently placed metal bleachers next to the wall where you could climb up and watch the animals. We lingered for just a few minutes while Ellie clambered over them.

Ellie, afraid of nothing and interested in everything, climbed to the very top and then back down. We kept an eye on her but she was nimble and things were fine. Until she got to the last step. In the blink of an eye, she took a graceful leap, misjudged the landing, slipped to the side, and bashed her head against the metal corner of the step above.

Blood was everywhere.

Ellie was screaming.

Our friends ran for help as we scrambled to pick up our little girl. One brought some paper napkins we had in the stroller. Another brought a zoo employee. As calmly as I could, I explained the situation in Spanish. The employee helpfully took us to the vet station not far away.

By this time, Ellie was beginning to calm. Inside the veterinary office, a kind animal doctor took over, seating Ellie on an examination table and taking a look at her head. I translated as the sweet man told her that he had treated the tiger on this very table. He stopped the bleeding and put a bandage on her head. He told me the cut wasn't too deep but that he highly recommended she get stitches. Since this had happened on zoo property, he wanted to call an ambulance and have them take us to the children's hospital right away. Wanting to be responsible parents and not having a better plan, we agreed.

It's important to understand that in the major cities of Argentina you can find excellent health care. By that time, I had already delivered one baby by c-section and had had gall-bladder surgery in one of their wonderful hospitals. It's also important to understand that, as a country with universal health care, Argentina has two kinds of hospitals. Public hospitals, which are free, and private hospitals, which accept medical insurance or cash. Previously, we had only used the latter.

On that day, the ambulance automatically took us to the former.

The public children's hospital in La Plata does a great deal of good for kids who would otherwise not be able to afford health care. It is clean and staffed by qualified doctors and nurses. It is also crowded beyond belief.

We waited for an hour just to tell someone what had happened. By now, bandaged and feeling better, Ellie was more annoyed by the wait than the head wound. Still, we had been advised that she would have a terrible scar on her face without stitches, so we stuck it out. Another hour passed and we were finally called back to the treatment area. Only one adult was allowed to accompany the patient. I went. Nate waited outside.

I should explain that living in a foreign country brings up a lot of difficult choices, but one of the biggest is how you will handle the language. Nate and I were fortunate.

Because we had started young, we both spoke Spanish fluently, having studied it in school and then lived in Argentina for months at a time before we got married. Even so, the language you grow up speaking (in our case, English) is the language of your heart, and communication in marriage is hard enough without introducing the complication of a foreign language. So we had made the decision early on to speak English to one another at home and Spanish everywhere else.

When we had the kids, we did the same. They were exposed to Spanish constantly in public and when guests were over, but within our family, we spoke English. The result was that in the early years when they spent most of their day with us, they didn't really speak Spanish at all. It wasn't until Ellie started preschool that she began to understand what native speakers were saying. Even then, it took years.

After we moved back to the US a few years later, we were thankful for our decision. That day in the children's hospital? Not so much.

When Ellie's name was called, we followed a nurse down the linoleum hallway to the brightly lit room with the metal table. There were four women in the room. I assumed one was a doctor and the other three were nurses or assistants of some kind. It wasn't made clear. They made Ellie lie down and explained that they were going to sterilize the wound. I translated, inserting reassurances that this part wouldn't hurt. They were just going to take off the bandage and rub something cold on it. Ellie was already stiff as a board and began crying frantically the moment they took the bandage off. They told her to lie still. I translated. She didn't. They held her down. I told her in English what they were doing. She screamed.

Then the worst and most unimaginable thing happened. One of the nurses told me it was time for me to leave.

"I can't leave," I said. "She doesn't speak Spanish. She doesn't know what you're saying to her. I need to translate."

"You have to step into the hall," she said, physically herding me in that direction. "This is a surgical procedure. Parents can't be in the room."

Ellie was screaming. The women were holding her down, telling her that it was going to be okay and that she just needed to hold still. She couldn't understand them.

"She can't understand you! I need to stay! It's just a couple of stitches!"

"No," the woman said. By now she had pushed me into the hall and was blocking the door as I tried to return.

Ellie called for me. "Mommy! Mommy! I need you!"

I tried to push past the nurse. She was an immovable rock.

I could hear Ellie scream as the stitches began. She was calling my name between screams. The irritated nurses were telling her to calm down. In Spanish.

I tried to shout around the horrible woman in my way, telling Ellie I was right outside and that it would be over soon. I don't think she heard me over her own yelling.

My hands curled into fists. Not that I would actually punch anyone, mind you, but it never hurts to be prepared.

I'm sure it only took about three minutes, but it felt like hours before Nurse Ratched moved and I could run to Ellie's side, could hug her close, could tell her that it was all over.

I was shaking and crying. Ellie was crying and clinging to me. I picked her up, and they hurried us out of the room so the next person could be seen.

Somewhere along the way, someone gave Ellie a lollipop. By the time we joined Nate in the outer waiting room, she was calmly licking it, already putting the experience behind her.

I cried all the way home.

Ten years later, Ellie has a tiny scar on her forehead. The scar on my psyche is much bigger.[1] Having someone physically prevent me from going to my child when she

---

[1] Ellie told me recently that she remembers that day vividly. I have to tell you that it broke my heart a little. She's fine, really. Totally fine. But I had comforted myself for so long by imagining that she would quickly forget.

was screaming for me is still in the top three worst moments of my life. Even though it was only a minor wound. Even though everything worked out fine. After all these years, I can't think about that moment without feeling sick inside. As I type this, I'm wiping tears out of my eyes.

What is it that happens to us when we become parents?

I've never been much into the mystical magic of motherhood. Birthing a child did not suddenly give me supernatural intuition or transform me into a selfless nurturer. I still rely on my brain rather than my gut, and I still think babies are boring. But, friends, I would throw myself in front of a speeding train to save my kids from being hurt. I wouldn't even think twice.

And yet, they do get hurt. All kids do. They fall and skin a knee or break an arm or get a concussion. Their friends trample their feelings or random strangers at school make them cry. They experience disappointment, they experience failure, they experience loss. And every single time I see my kids hurt, it hurts me inside, too. Nothing makes me lose sleep like knowing they are in pain.

As far as I can tell, this never stops. So much that I never fully knew about my own mother is clear to me now. How personal my struggles are to her. How she feels the weight of anything I suffer. When Scott had an emergency appendectomy a few years ago, she sat with me in the waiting room, concerned about him, concerned about me, and it suddenly hit me. Now her pain in motherhood has been multiplied. She feels her grandchildren's pain and she feels her children's pain, and it's all added to her own. This burden of loving only gets heavier with time.

This is a thing my kids don't understand, and that's just as well. When they are hurting, the last thing I want them to be concerned with is how it's hurting me. But I do hope that in some way, they can sense that they aren't alone in their pain.

It's not that their suffering can be divided. It's not that I can make it any less. Pain is not an equation. It's just that their pain matters. To at least one person in the world, the hurt they experience is as personal and as visceral as it is to them.

They will have to fight their own battles in their own way. But wherever I am, however far away, while I draw breath, they will never be fighting alone.

I don't know why God allows so much pain to be a part of this world he made. I can't speak to his plan for the universe. But in Isaiah, he tells his people that he will comfort them as a mother comforts her children, and I think maybe I do understand what that means.

It's not the comfort of taking away the pain. It's not the comfort of answers, and it's not the comfort of revenge.

It's the comfort of someone whose whole heart is for us, someone who feels acutely everything we go through. It's the comfort of knowing that we matter, that our pain matters, and that the burden of loving us will gladly be carried for eternity.

We all still have to fight our own battles in our own way, but we're never, ever fighting alone.

Honestly, that's not always the kind of comfort I want, but it just might be the comfort that I need.

15

I'm Made Out of Dirt. What Did You Expect?

When I was thirty-five, my life path took a sudden sharp turn. I already had three kids and a very badly-behaved hound dog, and in the span of a few months, I went from badass working mom in the slums of South America to slightly befuddled stay-at-home mom in a subdivision in Indianapolis. The transition was abrupt and stressful.

My kids were six, four, and two.[1] In those first few weeks back, we needed to find a house, enroll Ellie in first grade, find a preschool for Scott, and purchase things like beds to sleep in and dishes to eat off of. House hunting and paperwork and phone calls to new medical providers filled my days. At night, I worried about the weird little things, like the fact that all my kids had abruptly stopped drinking milk because it tasted different here. In my rare moments alone, I would sit on the floor of my in-laws' house, feeling tense from head to

---

[1] The hound dog was also two, in case you were wondering. Or, I suppose, 14 in dog years. Either way, he had not outgrown his tendency to be a pain in the butt.

toe as if my muscles could trap all of the stress in my body, could keep it from bubbling out like hot lava and burning everyone I loved.

I remember those first weeks in snapshots.

We found a house to rent, but they wouldn't let us sign the lease in time to register for school. I held the stress in while I talked to the school secretary. She kindly allowed me to use the new address and bring the paperwork later. The following Tuesday, I drove Ellie to our soon-to-be new street to meet the bus. When I dropped her off she held my hand, but not too tightly. I remembered the anxiety I felt on her first day of all-Spanish preschool and breathed a sigh of relief that this time she'd at least understand her teacher. When I picked her up at the end of the day, she threw herself into my arms shouting, "I love, love, love school!"

The tiniest bit of the tightness eased in my core.

The price of preschool was a bit of a blow, but I held the stress in as I wrote the first check. Scott and Lucy and I spent many afternoons at thrift stores and garage sales. I bought kitchen utensils and bedsheets, and they goggled over the awesome selection of used toys everywhere. One night after dinner, the three of us spent ten minutes belly-laughing over the many hilarious ways to say the word "pinchy." Later, when I tucked Scott in bed, he looked up and said, completely out of the blue, "Mommy, you know the only way to really walk on water is to keep looking at Jesus. I know that because it says it in the Bible. Remember that story with Peter?"

I breathed in, and it didn't hurt quite as much as before.

Eventually, we moved into our new house. We had friends over and sat on the floor because we still had no chairs. The kids played in the backyard, and tree shadows made patterns on the walls, and we talked and laughed, and it was a promise that there would be joy in this new life, too.

It was a long time before I felt the full realization of that promise, many months and even years before I could be at peace with all that had happened and have a sense of who I was meant to be here.

In the meantime, I was a mom. Some days I felt good, and we played in the yard and baked cookies and sang songs. Some days, I was not so much okay, and I supervised naps and cut up apples and told stories with my brain on autopilot.

And some days, I laid on my bed during naptime and stared out at the trees in the backyard, not really thinking but, just breathing. Often on those days, when naptime ended, I didn't have any playing in me, and we piled up on the couch and watched TV instead.

I doubt my kids noticed much difference between one day and another. They were young and well-loved, and I was struggling with the kind of existential problem that wouldn't even have made sense to them. But their oblivious happiness made a difference. It brought me joy. It refocused me on what mattered.

Then and now, to be a source of comfort to me, they only have to exist.

A couple of years ago, after a particularly hard week, I was crying on the couch when I thought everyone else was busy. Lucy came in and crept close when she saw my tears.

"What's wrong, Mommy?" she asked.

"I'm sad, baby," I said. "It's nothing you did. I'm just really sad, and right now I need to cry for a little bit."

She didn't answer, just crawled up and stretched out on top of me, laying her head on my chest. I cried for a while more, while my baby hugged me.

As much as we wish it, we can't always be the picture of strength for our kids. We can't always keep a stiff upper lip. We can't always pull it together.

Sometimes chronic health issues plague us, and our bodies simply can't do what we think they should. Sometimes disaster strikes, and the trauma is more than we can bear. Sometimes all the stress cannot be contained.

The shame of not being strong enough and the anger of life putting us in this position can combine to choke us. Why does it have to be so hard? And why can I not be better than this?

I am convinced that God, that father who knows things we couldn't understand even if he told us, brings us to those places on purpose. He knows something important and knows that we won't believe it unless we see it for ourselves.

When I am weak, then I am strong. His strength is made perfect in my weakness.

This is parenting. This wrestling with our own emotions right there in front of our children. Winning the struggle sometimes, and sometimes losing, too.

This is parenting. This enduring the failings of our bodies. This battling to bear pain with fortitude and weakness with grace. Winning the battle sometimes, and sometimes losing, too.

I have come to believe that my struggling is God's mercy to my children. That when their own turn comes, they will know that this is a thing that happens. That they are not broken, just made out of ordinary dirt by a hand that knew exactly what it was doing.

That, like me, they are weak, but that in their weakness they can find the source of all strength.

16

I'm Terrible With Numbers, But I've Got Your Six

Long before Nate was my husband or fiancé or boyfriend or even romantic interest, he was my best friend.[1]

The short version of a story that starts when I was sixteen and is still going on today is that we met on a summer mission trip. I thought he was overwhelmingly intense and overly serious but still somehow one of those people who just got it in the ways that mattered. We became friends, and we wrote letters for the next year.[2] He took me to a concert just as friends on my 18th birthday. We ended up at the same college, gathered a group of friends and proceeded to hang out constantly

---

[1] Though come to think of it, I'm not sure that I ever referred to him as my boyfriend. That phase was just so...short.

[2] Real, honest-to-God paper letters because it was 1993 and we lived on opposite sides of the country. Yes, I still have them, but no, you can't read them. There's a limit to my willingness to humiliate myself.

for the next several years. In my last semester, when I was student teaching, my car died, so my good friend Nate let me borrow his Taurus every day to drive to school. We'd meet up at night to pass off the car, talk for an hour or two, and be as dumb as two smart people can be about what it meant that those two hours were the best part of every day. Finally, on Halloween of 1998, we admitted the possibility of a different kind of relationship. Two months later we were engaged, and we got married the next June.[3]

The day before we started dating was a perfect snapshot of our friendship to that point. It was October 30, and our college was throwing a huge "Halloween Fun Fest." As the student body president, Nate needed to attend, and he needed to attend in costume. He called me that morning and asked for help putting something together.

We spent the day driving around between thrift stores and Wal-Mart, piecing together a Winnie the Pooh costume from old clothes and costume ears and face paint. We were both epically bad at making things, but

---

[3] For the record, I absolutely have always believed in dating as a concept even though I never really did it much. After taking myself too seriously for teenage relationships, I skipped the hard and usually necessary parts, and married my best friend when I was only 22. I truly wish that everyone could have such an uncomplicated path, but I know it's not something you can manufacture. I did my best to make wise choices, but I don't fool myself about how much luck was involved.

we didn't give up until we had overcome every obstacle and laughed our way through every problem.

The resulting Pooh Bear was downright terrifying, which isn't really what we were going for, but Nate pulled it off with his usual confidence. As for me, I deftly downplayed my role in its creation.

You wouldn't think blowing an entire Saturday to make the world's ugliest costume would be fun, but we both agreed it was the best day we'd spent in a long time. I guess that's how you finally admit you're in love with someone. If you're willing to make a travesty of a beloved children's character just to be together, you can pretty much assume the rest of life is going to be better together, too.

It was.

In the early years of our marriage, before we moved to Argentina, before we had kids, when we had not yet been married long enough for people to stop giving us the patronizing "oh, you're just newlyweds" smile, we had a lot of naïve ideas and grandiose plans. Some of them were solid and some were silly, but there was one thing we had completely dead to rights.

We wanted to build a very specific kind of life, and we were one hundred percent, friend-that-sticks-closer-than-a-brother, put-your-back-on-me in it together.

And by "it," I mean everything.

The life we were after wasn't his life that I was going along with. It wasn't my life that he was making possible. It was our life, our dreams, our work, our family, our legacy.

People thought we were adorable.[4]

I remember a conversation we had with my dad not long before we moved to Argentina. We were waxing on about how we looked at our job as OUR job and how we planned to be full partners in it,[5] and my dad said, "That will be wonderful...until you have kids."

"Why would it change when we have kids?" Nate asked.

"Well, someone will have to take care of them. At some point the work will have to be primarily one person's work so that the other person can focus on the family. It's just practical. What will you do if you both have to meet with someone at the same time? Who will stay home with the kids?"

"We'll take turns. We'll reschedule. We'll prioritize." The answers were right there. It seemed so obvious to us.

---

[4] And, I mean, obviously we were, but not in the condescending way that they thought.

[5] Which I grant you, was probably pretty annoying, but it was important to us. And also, dang it, we were right.

"Okay," my dad said, clearly unconvinced but also not wanting to argue. "We'll see what happens."

So we did. We did the work and then we had the kids, and sure enough, it was crazy complicated, just as my dad predicted.

But before Nate was my husband, my coworker, or the father of my kids, he was my best friend, the one who wanted what I wanted, the one I counted on, the one who always had my back.

We did what we had said we'd do. We took turns. We rescheduled. We prioritized. We also took kids along with us, did jobs together, and skipped what we had to skip. We talked. All the time. We dreamed and we complained and we problem-solved and we despaired and we analyzed. We had each other's backs. We made sacrifices, not so much for each other as for the common life we were trying to build.

We have never (in over twenty years of being married and over fifteen of being parents) changed our minds about being full and equal partners in our life. Massive life and job changes have led to shifting responsibilities and different divisions of labor, but the life we are still building is one life. It's our life. Together.

Now that my kids are teenagers, I can see how this common purpose that stabilizes us is also an incredible gift to them. They are growing up as a central part of a life that was chosen, that is chosen every day. They are not distractions from that life or addendums to it, but they are also not the totality of that life. They are important characters in a story that started before they appeared on the scene and will continue after they leave to write their own stories. They matter (so much that it can't be put into words but only felt in the bones) but the weight of this narrative doesn't rest on their shoulders.

It's a gift to be a part of something bigger than yourself.

It's a gift I recommend to every young parent or parent-to-be. Build a life, know your purpose, work at it side-by-side with your spouse, and do whatever it takes. Then bring your kids into that and let them make it even better.

And when that isn't possible? What then? I am acutely aware that a marriage based on common purpose isn't everyone's experience. People get married for all kinds of reasons. There are hormones, social pressures, economic needs, and questionable advice. There is abuse and deception and false teaching. There are just plain mistakes. People also get married thinking that they share a common purpose only to find out that their partner was dishonest or enslaved to addictions they knew nothing about. You don't know what you don't know, and then when you do, you're already a long way down the road.

My friend Marta was the first to teach me that.[6]

---

[6] Not her real name. Some stories are only partially mine.

When we moved to Argentina, we were there to learn how to start new church communities in neighborhoods that had none, so our mentors connected us with a family living on the south side of Buenos Aires. Alberto was a skilled machinist, but like a quarter of the men living in his neighborhood at that time, he was out of work. Marta was a stay-at-home mother of three kids, who took them on the train to school every day and then hustled at any small jobs she could to help make ends meet. They had recently started a Good News Club for neighborhood kids, and they'd been hoping for a long time to start a church there. In many ways, we had nothing in common with them, but they seemed like people who wanted to build what we wanted to build. And they seemed like people who had each other's backs.

For about a year, Nate and I traveled from our city apartment by bus or train nearly every day out to the neighborhood where this family lived. We helped with the kids' club, visited families, shared meals and long conversations with our new teammates. Working so closely together helped us clarify what we wanted to be doing. By undisputed mutual agreement, after that year, we left our apartment and moved into the neighborhood.[7] The move was massively stressful. Our new apartment was a complete disaster. But I knew that if I was all alone figuring out how to clean grease off the kitchen walls, it was because Nate was down the hall learning how to

---

[7] Because, as Nate put it, it made no sense to move 10,000 miles to do something and then fail because you wouldn't move the last ten.

repair broken blinds. If the power shorted out—which it did on the regular—I would light the gas stove while he called the landlord to get the key to the fuse box. Building the life we wanted was hard beyond what we had imagined, but we were doing it together, and that made all the difference.

In the meantime, we were learning how rare that kind of teamwork really is. Working with Alberto and Marta was complicated. Cross cultural relationships are always hard, and ours was made even more challenging by our youth and lack of experience and their stressful life situation. We learned that you can say the same words for what you want but mean totally different things. We learned that you have to listen with more than just your ears if you want to understand. We learned that doing really hard work with people takes an immense amount of trust, and we learned that trust like that takes a long time to build. These lessons were all painfully slow in coming, but each step forward felt like a victory.

Two years into our work there, a little community was forming, our relationship with Alberto and Marta had developed a workable rhythm, and I was pregnant with our first baby. It seemed like things were stable enough, and we went home to the US for a couple of months to visit the people who supported us and let Ellie be born near family.

Three days before Ellie's due date, we got a call from our mentor in Argentina. Earlier that morning, Marta had hanged herself in the upstairs of their house. She was still clinging to life at the time of the call, but she died in the hospital two days later.

My world was rocked. Nate got on a plane to go be with Alberto, and some friends came and stayed with me as I cried out all my horror and grief and as I prayed fervently that my daughter wouldn't be born until her dad came back.[8]

Life continued, as it always impossibly does after tragedy. Over the course of the next months and years, we continued to work in that neighborhood, to take care of Alberto and the kids, and to listen to those who knew Marta best. As we did, the picture of her intense loneliness became clear. Marta was wrestling with life-long demons, and despite outward appearances, no one had her back. A couple of years later, Alberto's actions revealed more of his character, and we realized that he had not been Marta's partner in building the life she wanted. Things weren't what they looked like. She was on her own, and alone is exactly the place where lies sound the most convincing.

In the end, she believed the lies. It's one of the great griefs of my life that I was not old enough, wise enough, or present enough to speak the truth she needed to

---

[8] She wasn't. Not only did she wait until his return, she waited until we were ten days past her due date and the doctors induced, and even then she wouldn't come out without an emergency C-section. Can prayers ever be too effective?

counteract those lies. Maybe it wouldn't have mattered. Maybe she wouldn't have listened, couldn't have listened. I know her life didn't depend on me. But I can't see it as a coincidence that her ultimate moment of despair came when her teammates were half a world away. And while I don't blame myself, I will always feel the heartbreak of that.

Because I know that not everyone has a spouse to have their back, but I also know that doesn't have to mean that they are alone. When God adopted us as his children, he made us into a family, and he gave us all a chance to have partners in building our lives, brothers and sisters, uncles and aunts, mothers and fathers who can speak truth and provide support and be something bigger for us and our children to be a part of.

In the years since Marta's death, I have known other men and women whose life partners did more destroying than building, and I have seen what can happen when they are able to fall back onto this family and find life.

I have a dear friend who found herself abandoned several years ago with traumatic suddenness. She responded by opening her life wide to her friends. A band of women took turns coming to sleep on her couch every single night for months while she recovered from her shock and loss. A whole community stepped in and watched children and shopped for groceries and gave space for her to rebuild a life that was hers. It isn't the life she imagined when she was young and it isn't everything she ever could have dreamed, not yet, at least. But it is hers, a life built on the things that matter to her, a life of hard work and friendship, of safe and loving places for her children, of generosity and counsel and care for other people in need. It's a beautiful life, a life in process like all of our lives, a life where people have her back. It's a life that she is giving as a gift to her children as much as Nate and I are doing the same for ours.

For all the hard and awful things I've found in the world, I never stopped being amazed at how wide open life is, how many different ways there are for it to be wonderful.

Thank God we each get to make our own kind of just right.

And thank God we never have to do it alone.

Part 3

Laughing With My Community

17

The Grass Is Always Greener Where The Fertilizer's Been Spread Thick

By the time I graduated high school, I had attended nine different schools in four different states. That sounds crazy, and maybe it was, but like every kid, I thought my life was normal. And there were legitimate benefits to all the moving. I didn't know it then, but I now realize that my childhood was a crash course in cultural adaptation.

The summer before second grade, my family moved from northern California to a small military town in Oklahoma. It was hard to find my footing as the new girl in my class. When newness is the only thing people know about you, it's easy to feel invisible. For the first few months, I put my head down and focused on something I knew I could master: my schoolwork.

The second week of school, my teacher announced that we would begin to have weekly spelling tests. My ears perked up at the chance to prove myself. I was an excellent speller. She handed out blank paper for the weekly pre-test, and then she began to recite the words. The idea was that we would write them down as we thought they were spelled and then find out how much we needed to study before the real test on Friday.

She walked through the room as she said the words out loud, and I wrote each one in the full confidence that I was already getting them right. I can still feel myself sitting in that little student desk as she got to number eight.

"Hee-all," she said, pausing before repeating. "Hee-all."

I paused, not sure if she meant "heal" or "heel." She hadn't given a sentence to clarify. Determined not to be counted wrong on this test that didn't count for anything, I wrote it both ways to demonstrate the completeness of my knowledge.

A few minutes later, she went over the test. As I thought, I had nailed them all. Until number eight.

"Hee-all," she said again. "H-I-L-L."

I looked at her. I looked at my paper. I looked at her again. She and her southern accent had already moved on to number nine. Furtively, I scribbled out my wrong answer and hoped that no one had noticed that I misspelled the easiest word of all time.

But really, lady, if you expect us to know that you're walking up a "heel," the least you can do is use the word in a sentence. We're not all from Oklahoma.

This book is not an autobiography, so I won't spend too much time on the details of all my childhood moves and school changes. Suffice it to say that my immediate family was stable and happy, but our life was uprooted often and for a variety of reasons. My brother and I reacted quite differently to that aspect of our childhood, so I won't claim that my feelings are representative of all kids, but for me, starting a new life on a regular basis felt exciting and, though stressful, still desirable. I developed a dread of stagnation. I would hear people talk about living in the same house for forty years and I would shudder. I couldn't imagine anything more depressing.

Unsurprisingly, I moved halfway across the country to go to college. I spent winter break of my junior year helping my parents move again. The final summer of college, I studied abroad in South America. When Nate and I first talked about getting married, he told me he was planning to do his post-grad internship in Argentina, which would mean living there for at least a year. I couldn't think of anything more perfect.

I can sincerely say that when we moved to Buenos Aires a month before I turned twenty-five, I really wanted to serve God and love other people. But if I'm honest, I was also excited by the adventure of it all. I was inspired by the idea of a fresh start on an even more epic scale than I had experienced before. There was so much about life in America (and church in America) that I found distasteful, and I dreaded a future of trying to make slow improvements to the faulty structures I saw around me. It seemed more efficient and desirable to go far away, to build something new from the ground up.

151

I mean, if I was in it from the beginning, I could do it right, start with a firm foundation, you know?

Obviously, that was both incredibly arrogant and incredibly naive. I'd blame it on my youth—I'm not the first twenty-something to underestimate the problems in the world and overestimate my own abilities—but honestly, I know people of all ages who are convinced that the best plan is to pick up and run when things aren't the way they ought to be. Feeling unhappy in your current house? Time to move. Job getting frustrating? Get a new one. Friends not living up to expectations? Find other friends.

Fixing things is hard. Walking away seems easier.

That appearance is a delusion. Yes, sometimes walking away is necessary. Some things do get broken beyond repair. After some journeys you can't go home again. In those cases, starting over is the brave choice, but the reason it requires courage is that it is never, ever, ever easy.

After our first tragedy in Argentina, we returned to our work with sober hearts and full hands. Ellie was four months old, and the joy of her fresh new life was echoed by the wonderful rebirth that seemed to be happening around us. Our tiny new community had pulled together after our teammate Marta's suicide. They rallied around Alberto and the children. Many of the ladies pitched in to do housework or provide childcare. As we worked together, we grew closer. This was community as I had dreamed it would be.

A handful of women started meeting every week to read Bible stories and talk about what they meant for our life. Most of the group had very little education, but they loved those stories, often retelling them at home to their husbands and children. One of my friends was particularly thriving, and over time, I began to ask her to do the storytelling. By then, I was pregnant with Scott, and when his due date arrived, I let them know I'd be missing our gathering for several weeks, but I knew they were in good hands, each other's hands.

Scott's birth was a dream. After the first week of inverted days and nights, he settled down to being the easiest little baby I could have asked for.[1] When the requisite time went by, I was eager to get back to meeting with the other women, and I was happy to discover that even with two children, I'd still be able to manage it.

The first day I showed up, I knew something was wrong. A few people were missing, and tension hung in the air between those who were there. I tried to ask what was happening, but no one was willing to admit to any problem. I went home worried and confused.

The next week, no one came.

The week after, we got a call from a young man who was interning with us that year. He'd been talking to one of

---

[1] Well, not that little, I guess. He was a chunky nine pounds at birth, and at least two of them must have been in his cheeks.

our kids and the story had come out. A married woman in our group was accusing Alberto, our recently widowed teammate, of making inappropriate advances toward her, and everyone was divided over whether it was true or false.

We began to deal with the situation as quickly and openly as possible. At first, it was hard to determine how serious the offense had been, but then another woman came forward with similar accusations and a letter he had written full of the same kind of inappropriate things he'd been saying. Confronted with the letter, he continued to insist that none of it was wrong. He openly lied about events that had occurred even when it was obvious that he wasn't telling the truth. It was devastating.

There is nothing more destructive than someone in a position of trust who takes advantage of the people that trust him. All summer it was like an earthquake had hit our little community. In the end, though much love was still expressed on an individual level, the community scattered. The work we had poured our hearts into for nearly five years was gone just like that.

In addition to the grief of personal loss, it was a painful lesson in our own powerlessness.

There was no finding a silver lining in the dark clouds that descended that year. After the community dissolved, one man, Mario, came and asked Nate to continue working with him and teaching him. He was a good friend and his dedication seemed like a hopeful seed for the future. Then a month later, Mario was struck by a car and killed.

Friends, there's no such thing as a fresh start where everything goes right the first time. Wherever you go, there you are, and there darkness is, too. Some that you brought with you and some that was waiting when you arrived. Both as inevitable as the setting sun.

We had all the right ideas, all the right principles, all the right strategies for building a community, and it still ended in disaster. My fresh start was as flawed and frustrating as all those existing communities I had seen and rejected. And now I knew that while I could have a new start in a new place, it wasn't going to fix the fundamental problems.

We could have given up on the idea of community altogether. If people are that flawed and fragile everywhere, that prone to hurting each other, what's even the point in trying to bring them together? But the persistence of darkness, inside us and among us, only makes our need for the light greater. Instead of hoping to find some people in some place where the darkness wouldn't be so strong, we had to figure out how to adapt to life wherever we were surrounded by tough, weird humans that made a mess of everything.

Having babies helped me make that shift in my thinking. Because my "fresh start" wasn't working out as imagined in my little family, either. When I had pictured having kids, I had high hopes of shaping their little lives from day one, reading to them *en utero* and playing imaginative games, teaching life lessons with serene wisdom and singing them into pleasant dreams each night. Unsurprisingly, that's not exactly how things went.

All those books I was going to read out loud while pregnant? They got lost in the battle between morning sickness and carrying on with my job and life. The novels that we'd work through as they were babies? Shredded by a little girl who didn't want to be still for even a moment and whose emotional intensity left me so exhausted that all I could do was turn on the television.

Oh yes, friends, there was television. Just a half hour at first, and always something educational.[2] Then it was a show after every nap to ease her through the pain of waking up. Then it was no more than three hours of TV a day, and yes, fine, if you really want to watch another episode of *Fraggle Rock,* I suppose it could be worse.[3]

All of this created the most intense guilt in me. I grew up without a television, a decision my mom made intentionally for our well-being, and while my decision to have a TV was equally intentional, I felt like I was failing

---

[2] Remember *Baby Einstein*? We were their target audience. Man, those videos were mind-numbing, but who wouldn't suffer through shapes dancing to classical music if it was making your kid smarter?

[3] It couldn't be worse than *Fraggle Rock*, though. It really couldn't. There was a wisdom-dispensing *trash pile,* for heaven's sake. She sang.

every time I turned it on instead of going outside or doing a craft or putting a puzzle together.

But first of all, puzzles were a no-go from the start. I'm not exaggerating when I say that my kids are the smartest kids I know, but when I would hand them a puzzle piece, it was like an alien object. Why are you turning it upside down? Can't you see how this one has the same red hair as that one? You can't? I know you want it to fit together with the pink one, but it doesn't. No matter how hard you push on it, it's not going to lock together. Nope, not there either. OH MY WORD, THIS IS A TWENTY PIECE PUZZLE AND WE'VE BARELY DONE FIVE PIECES. Yes, we can put it away. Yes, Mommy would also like a snack. Mommy would like all the snacks.

Secondly, do you know how early small children wake up? If your gregarious preschooler is up by six a.m., naptime is literally a full workday away. That's a lot of hours to fill, and Ellie would not play by herself for a single one of them. We had breakfast. We went for a walk. We did a craft. We played with play dough. Then I would check the clock and it would be 8:30 am.

Now what? Now what, I ask you?

This is how grown adults came to accept the annoying voices of Caillou and Dora the Explorer. It was someone else to talk to our kids for a while.

Not only was I exhausted most days, my kids were not the clean slates I had expected to write truth and beauty on. From the beginning, they were complicated individuals with their own wills and their own hearts full of the same wonder and selfishness and determination that filled mine. They were — and are — orders of magnitude beyond my expectations in every way. More amazing and more difficult than I could have imagined.

As I said before, kids are tougher and weirder than you think. In my experience, this starts from the very first day. Kids don't become tough or become weird. Those things may increase or decrease over time, but they are baked in from day one, as if both resilience and oddity are part of the basic ingredients of humans.

So day after day, television show after television show, I came to accept my inability to create the perfect children, the perfect family. But I didn't give up on being a good mom. I got up and kept building with what I had. Most days back then, I didn't feel great about it, but I didn't run away either.

Nate and I didn't run away from our community either. We saw our people through to the end. We poured our remaining time in the neighborhood into caring for Mario's widow and five children. And when our work was no longer possible there and we eventually moved to a different neighborhood with a different team, we began to build the same kind of community again.

Not because this new community had any better chance of being perfect, but because tough, weird humans like us need community, and we couldn't help but build.

18

I Dealt With All The Other Messes, Now Where Do I Find The Bleach For My Brain?

My third and final baby spent a lot of her infancy on the floor. I'm not even going to apologize for it.

Lucy was born right at the beginning of the current baby-wearing trend, and since we lived in another country and were at least ten years behind all trends, I didn't have any nifty slings or wraps. I had one very uncomfortable "baby backpack" that contrasted starkly with the many cute baby blankets that could be tossed on the floor for Lucy to roll around on.

And she was just so happy to lay there and look at the world go by.

There were always things to watch. A whirlwind of a big sister. A snugly big brother. A puppy exactly six months older than she was and very interested in dashing about licking things.[1] Guests in and out. Noise and action in the neighborhood. More than enough stimulation for one introverted baby.

When Lucy learned to crawl, she was right there on the floor to have all the room she needed to do so. She explored our tiny house right next to the pup, slowly going after the things she had formerly just observed. She wasn't particularly adventurous, but at home, where she was familiar with everything in sight, she owned her world.

Which is how she began the habit of sticking her fingers in every crack and crevice to see what was hidden there. The door frames and window wells. The space under the couch. Behind the TV.

I think that last one is where she found the dead cockroach.

But then, does it matter where she found it? What matters is that I walked into the room to see my sweet little baby girl on the verge of putting a dead roach into her sweet little baby mouth.[2]

---

[1] If you question the sanity of taking on a puppy while you are pregnant with your third child, you are wise, and I wish I had known you eleven years ago.

[2] Please note that in Argentina, roaches grow to prodigious sizes, so this sucker was as big as her hand. You're welcome for that mental image.

I have never moved so fast in my life. I have never touched a roach so willingly, either. But I'm proud to say that I stopped her just in time.

Then I washed her hands and my hands and swept under and behind every piece of furniture in the house. I only wished there was some way to wash the memory from my brain.

If you've ever worried about the germs your child is exposed to or felt guilty about not keeping your house as clean as you should, congratulations. You now know that you are not doing as badly as you could be.

In all seriousness, though, while I still cringe when I think about that day, it's only a drop in the bucket of dirt and germs that my kids encountered daily. During their early years, we lived in neighborhoods on the edges of those temporary shanty-towns you see on the news. Ellie wore the sweet little dresses her grandparents bought her to play on the cement floors and packed dirt yards of her neighborhood friends. We took walks next to the open drainage ditches that lined our streets, and when the rain made drainage back up into our house, the water smelled of sewage. Sometimes we'd be without water for hours or even days at a time, which meant no bathing or, you know, flushing toilets. Yes, that *is* as bad as it sounds.

I don't say any of that to evoke pity or scorn or admiration or any particular response. It was just a fact of life where we lived, as it is for millions of people around the world. We did what everyone does: the best we could. I tried to keep my kids away from the open sewers and mostly succeeded. If I failed, I gave them a bath. I bathed them regularly, even though it was usually in a Rubbermaid tub. I made them eat their vegetables and drink their milk, and when we got food poisoning from the *choripan* we bought on the side of the road, we drank a lot of Gatorade and got through it.[3]

Once, our teammates rescued a tiny kitten from a nearby field. Our kids all loved that cat. They played with it. They snuggled it. We didn't discover that it had ringworm until all three families on our team were infected.[4] I spent the weeks before Lucy was born spreading cream over everyone in an attempt to get the red splotches totally healed before we had an infant in the house. It *almost* worked. The tiny spot on my right arm didn't disappear quite quickly enough, and while nursing Lucy, I transferred the fungus to her sweet newborn head. I know, right? But in the end, we went back to the pharmacy, got more cream, and a few weeks later, she was healed.

---

[3] *Choripan,* for those not privileged to have eaten it, is Argentine chorizo inside a piece of fresh bread. Every other corner in Buenos Aires has a man cooking some, alongside other amazing meats, on a repurposed barrel grill, and it is so delicious that even after it has made you sick a few times, you still find yourself stopping to buy some on a sunny Saturday. And by you, obviously, I mean me.

[4] If you aren't familiar with ringworm it's not *quite* as bad as it sounds. There are no worms involved. Just a fungal infection that is highly contagious and takes an act of God to eliminate.

Every time something like that happened, I felt all the sickening feelings of disgust and shame that you might imagine. I don't think anyone is so laid-back that they get to escape the disgust and shame. But whatever we might feel, we parents are the ones in charge of dealing with the mess. So we do the next thing. And then the next. And then the next.

As far as I can tell, that's really all there is to adulting. It's not knowing what you're doing. It's not being prepared or having a plan. It's figuring out the next step and then doing it, even when you feel like crawling into a hole and giving up.

For what it's worth, all these years later my kids are wonderfully healthy.

I could try to take credit for that. I could say that it was *because* I exposed them to so many germs that they have strong immune systems. Or that it was because I brought them home to a cleaner environment partway through their lives that we avoided the worst dangers. But I don't think either thing is true.

I know kids who lived in those slums who had asthma from the pollution and chronic health issues from malnutrition. I also know kids in the same exact households who licked ashes off of rusty nails when their parents weren't looking and grew up as strong and healthy as the proverbial horses. I know kids in middle-class America who have life-threatening allergies and others who have almost died from complications of the flu. I also know some who can run three miles without breaking a sweat and scarcely ever have so much as a cold.

It turns out that the human body, like everything else in life, is incredibly complex. Its health is affected by such an intricate mix of genetics and environment and random chance that we would be arrogant to take too much credit when it goes well and foolish to take too much blame when it doesn't.[5]

I'm not saying I don't need to make healthy choices when I can or that it makes no difference what I do. Many parts of our life and health do lie within our control, and I certainly want to tip the odds in my favor if I can. I would be foolish to ignore the very clear things that fall within my control. I would suggest, though, that so much of my kids' well-being is not up to me. Some things I can't change and some things I can't predict, and when I lose sight of that, I put myself where I don't belong. I make myself the ultimate authority and judge, of myself or of others or both.

Maybe, like me, you have judged yourself to be bad at taking care of your kids' health. You feel anxious about your choices. You feel shame from the times you didn't do enough or do the right things. Or maybe, you feel great about the choices you make for your kid's health. Maybe you feel that their well-being is a badge of honor for you. Maybe you judge others for not doing enough or

---

[5] And let's be honest, we're prone to doing both.

not doing the right things. Maybe under your genuine concern you believe that if other parents just made different choices, better choices, their kids would be better off. Like yours.

We need each other. We need to hear each other's experience and sometimes ask each other's advice. We need to pool our knowledge and do our best to make wise and informed decisions. But we need to hold our combined knowledge in open hands, to acknowledge how very much we don't know, to reject the shame that makes us hide and the pride that makes us judge. Both things only serve to keep us apart.

It doesn't sound particularly high-minded, but in a fractured world, our physical vulnerability is one of the few things that we all truly have in common. However different our values, our customs, and our beliefs about the world, we all live in fragile bodies and navigate a world over which we don't have nearly as much control as we'd like.

You and I and the moms in rural Ghana and the moms in the slums of St. Petersburg and the moms in ritzy Fifth Avenue apartments all have children whose arms break when they fall, whose bodies are susceptible to viruses, and whose hair makes a welcome home to lice. We most certainly don't all have the same access to prevention and treatment of those things, but we all have to deal with them when they happen.

If we could learn to accept our mutual weakness, I believe we'd find it easier to give each other more grace, and give ourselves more grace, too. Our frailty is a place where we can meet with compassion. Our bodily pain is a reality we can feel with true empathy. Our gross physicality is a thing we can laugh about together.

And in that place of vulnerability, we can help each other find the strength to do the next thing.

And the next.

And the next.

19

They've Already Killed All the Monsters

A few years ago, Lucy went through a brief *Sophia the First* phase. I think that that show is still around, but if it isn't, just picture the most inane princess platitudes that Disney has to offer crammed into a twenty minute animated sugar rush. The plucky title character goes from ordinary girl to princess overnight when her mother marries a king, and Sophia has to find a way to be royalty alongside her irresponsible stepbrother and vain stepsister. It's kind of a nightmare, but it's the exact brand that appeals to American girls of a certain age.

Lucky for me, Lucy's interest in the show didn't last long. She's always had good taste, and even at age six, inanity bored her quickly. But her brief fandom did produce one of my favorite Lucy comments of all time. I was sitting in the other room trying not to hear the horrible dialogue, when Lucy came wandering in.

"Mommy," she said. "The thing about Amber is that she thinks it's all about being pretty. But she doesn't get it. It's about being kind…AND pretty."

I laugh out loud every time I think about that. It was such a Lucy statement. There's nothing shallow about my girl, but she doesn't see any reason why you can't mine the depths and be stylish at the same time.

This is one of the chief sources of eye rolling between my girls. To be girly or not to be girly. To follow any given trend or to buck it. To care how you look or carefully not to care.

I get it. A lot of it is probably caused by my example. I have a horror of being overly stereotypical, and my love/hate relationship with all things girly has lasted a lifetime. Still, I try to encourage Lucy's love of beauty and style, even when it doesn't match my own. Because twenty years ago, some wonderful women taught me a lesson that changed my perspective on this particular battle.

After college, while Nate was pursuing his graduate degree, I took a job teaching Spanish in a rural high school in northern Indiana. This place was literally and figuratively outside of my comfort zone. Though I had moved around a lot as a kid, I was mostly a west coast city girl, and my new school was a lonely monolith surrounded for miles by Midwestern cornfields. The FFA was the strongest club at the school, my students initially saw little purpose in learning Spanish, and my fellow teachers were older than me and established in the small-town life of our community.[1]

I knew I was only going to be there for two years, but I was idealistic enough to pour my heart into my work while it lasted. After being hired by a principal who didn't even take the time to verify that I spoke fluent Spanish, I decided my best bet was to create my own world in my classroom and do the most good that I could inside its four walls.

Fortunately, a couple of my fellow teachers didn't let me escape that easily. These two wonderful ladies taught French and English respectively. They loved God and loved their students. They had many years of experience. And they cared enough about me to take the initiative to draw me in.

They met once a week to pray for the school, and they invited me to join them. I went, but with trepidation at first. Other than our jobs, we didn't have anything in common. I wasn't sure I wanted to take things to another level. But week after week, those women won me over. At the meetings, in addition to praying for students, they would each write notes to various ones, using colored pens and embellishing the notes with stickers and drawings.

For me, feminine handwriting and decorative tidbits had always been firmly in the category of "things that lack substance and therefore are unimportant." They were

---

[1] FFA, for you west coast city girls, stands for Future Farmers of America.

fine for those who liked them, but utterly unnecessary. I was going to spend my time on things that really mattered.

Over the course of those years with my sweet fellow teachers, though, I saw the impact that their notes had on students. I saw how taking the time to make a beautiful space in the classroom or writing someone's name with colors and flourishes created an atmosphere where kids felt valued and at home. I didn't become a different person through the influence of those women, but I did buy a set of pens. I did learn to occasionally pause my relentless pursuit of more words and knowledge and substance and make something just for the sheer joy of its beauty.

From the values of women who weren't like me, I learned to value something truly important.

In my lifetime, I have met women and men with such a miraculous range of gifts and perspectives that I couldn't possibly enumerate them all. Those gifts have enriched my world and changed me for the better, even while I still remain myself.

This is what I think of when my daughters roll their eyes at each other's taste and call each other dramatic and cringe at each other's sense of humor. I think of the ways they are each responding to the world and putting good things into the world and how utterly wonderful it is that they are growing up in the same house with the same parents and still will each contribute something uniquely their own.

This is the key to family unity and the key to all community. Yes, we need to be unified, to be for each other, to work for common goals. But we are better off if we're not all the same. We need diversity, not the political buzzword, but a true spectrum of culture, of experience, of taste, of gifting, of vision.

Our world is a big, big world, and our God is completely outside of any experience even that world can give us. The beauty I can see on my own is so very limited. If any of us hope to know God and to appreciate the world he made, we have to collect many points of view, many ways of seeing and ways of being. We have to listen and to look and to learn. We have to keep expanding our view our whole lives long.

And it's not just the beauty of the world that is bigger than us. The darkness is, too. The battle against it has to be fought with more weapons than I have in my own arsenal. I never would have thought to fight the darkness with stickers. But what a wonderful thing that someone else did.

One afternoon, years ago, two-year-old Lucy wanted to play with Barbies.

Having loved my own Barbies as a little girl and eagerly hoarded tiny glittery shoes and traded away stuffed animals for miniature ball gowns, I understood the appeal. As an adult, though, I had some feminist qualms. I've lived long enough to be concerned about real issues like body image and female stereotypes.

171

Still, she was little and liked shiny things and make believe, and I liked making her happy, so I didn't withhold the Barbies. But I did doubt my choice.

We sat on the floor with the pile of dolls and clothing, and Lucy meticulously chose each outfit, rejecting my advice and opinions. When they were deemed sufficiently fabulous, I asked where they were going.

"To a party," she said, the "duh" unspoken but still very clear.

I tried not to read anything into the overly stereotyped way she had them fuss with their hair one last time before heading out on the town. I mean yes, pink was her favorite color, and yes she couldn't think of anything more important for her dolls to do than dance around in sequined dresses, but that probably didn't mean she was destined to be vapid, right?

Or did it? Had she so thoroughly absorbed cultural standards that she conformed to them without even knowing why? Had I already failed at protecting my daughter from the world's bizarre expectations of women? Suddenly, all my feminist fears were on full blast.

The dolls were just finishing a very bouncy dance when Lucy sat up and began to direct my movements.

"Now make them dance, Mommy, but watch out. Now monsters are attacking them! Kick the monsters! Fight them! Here! I have the dog!"

She produced Barbie's floofy pink poodle.

"Now the puppy is fighting the monsters! We're all fighting them! And here comes their dad!"

Ken appears, dressed business casual.

"Now he's fighting the monsters, too! But it's too late! They've already killed all the monsters!"

The pile of Barbies do a victory dance, along with their dog and their dad, but it's nothing compared to the victory dance inside my head. My daughter's Barbies might have spent two hours getting dressed for a party, but they kicked butt when they got there. Things were going to be okay. Apparently, even Barbies can be instruments of good in the right hands.

So yeah, some of us fight monsters wearing combat boots. Some of us fight them in Converse hightops. And some of us wear heels.

Isn't it awesome that no matter what we're wearing, we all get to kick butt together?

20

No One Will Ever Be As Entertained By Us As Us

When I still had just one baby and one on the way, someone told me about this cool new thing called a "blog." It was like keeping a journal online, they said, where everyone can read it. Cool, I thought, because I'm sure the whole world is just dying to hear about my daily life. "Extra! Extra! Toddler insists on going for three walks and then refuses to nap!" They'd be lining up to read all about it.

A few months later, though, several of my friends who also had small children pinged me on AIM.[1] They were starting blogs on this site called Xanga, and they wanted me to do it, too. We could all write updates and post pictures, and it would be a fun way to keep up with each other, since they lived in several different states and I lived in another hemisphere. It was probably the only

---

[1] If you don't know what that is, imagine texting but on a desktop computer with dialup internet. You had to make an appointment to both arrive at the same time, but once you were there, you could chat long distance for free!

thing that could have motivated me to try out this new trend. I didn't really have friends in Argentina who were at my stage of life and I desperately wanted contact with the outside world.

So, in the same month Scott was born, I created my first blog (not-so-cleverly but very appropriately named *nateanddeb* because that was our brand and always would be) and began to write about my days with a newborn and a two-year-old hell-raiser.

You know how sometimes God gives you something you never thought to ask for, an answer to a prayer you didn't need to pray until later? This blog was one of those things. I posted my first entry on September 2, 2006. Two months later, an unexpected phone call kicked off the worst year of my life to that point. Without the lifeline of our small circle of Xanga blogs, I don't know how I would have survived.

That was the year that I had my first experience with a serial liar, the year our first church community fell apart, the year our dear friend died and two months later we had to perform a funeral for a baby. It was the year we first acknowledged defeat and moved home to temporary lodgings while we figured out our next steps.

That year, writing about my life and reading what my friends wrote about theirs kept me sane. The effort of putting my reality into words helped me see it with more perspective. Knowing someone was reading and caring made me feel less alone. I could read about how my friends were grappling with life and work and small children, and it gave me context for my own struggles.

It also helped me find the humor in them. No one will ever be as entertained by my friends and I as we are by ourselves. It's how I know I have the right friends.

One Saturday, I wrote about how Ellie had woken me up early with her usual restless longing to go out, out, out into the world. I didn't have much energy for going, but holding back that hurricane child would have taken even more, so we put on our coats and headed toward the playground in the plaza. Outside, the air was chilly. We were the only ones on the street. In our neighborhood the weekends were for late night parties, and more people went to bed at 7 a.m. than woke up at that time.

At the playground, I let go of her hand and let her run free, watching carefully anytime she bent down to pick something up. Broken glass and cigarette butts were as plentiful as the sad tufts of grass, so some vigilance was required. She climbed the wooden slide and swung on the squeaky swings. I tried to focus on my radiant child and not on the dreary surroundings. But it was Saturday morning, and I was tired and sad. It hadn't been an easy few months.

Then my girl came running toward me with something small held in her pudgy hand. She held it up, this tiny living thing she had found. It was a scraggly flower, a weed really, but the small white blossom lifted my heart.

"Even here," I thought to myself, "Even here there is beauty."

Then I lifted up my eyes, looked over my daughter's head…and saw a man peeing into the bushes.

"Mommy," Ellie wanted to know as we walked home. "Why are you laughing?"

I couldn't explain, but I also couldn't stop.

There's nothing funny about your child being exposed to public urination, but that doesn't mean you won't giggle all the way home. And you'll definitely laugh out loud later when you're writing about it to your friends. Because sometimes you can find beauty in the middle of ashes, and sometimes, you just find absurdity and you have to make do.

This is one of my favorite things about laughter. It doesn't always have to make sense. You can laugh for good reasons or bad reasons or for no reason at all. Life gets overwhelming, and it's a relief to let your feelings out without having to understand them first.

A few years later, Nate and I checked into a hospital in La Plata for the scheduled c-section of our third child. We still didn't know if it was a boy or a girl, and this hospital was new to us, but we still felt relaxed in that way you do when you have a couple of experiences already under your belt.

We showed up at 7:00 on a Monday morning, received the promised private room, and a nurse came with the gown I was to put on before he escorted me down to the surgical floor. Nate asked if there were scrubs for him. The man blinked a few times before understanding.

"Oh no," he said, "you can't go into the operating room. You'll wait in the surgical waiting room."

We exchanged a glance that asked each other if we'd both heard the same thing. Some times Spanish is a tricky language, so you never know, right?

"I was in the operating room for both of my other children's deliveries," Nate explained.

"No," the nurse said. "It's hospital policy. Fathers aren't allowed in the OR. The waiting room is right outside. I'll show you."

My heart sank, but I was already in the delivery zone. I had come here to get this baby out of me, and I would do whatever it took to make that happen. There are moments for fighting the man, and then there are moments for letting the man make whatever stupid policies he wants as long as he gives you your baby safely and makes it so that you aren't pregnant any more.

I shrugged at Nate. He shrugged at me. "Lead the way."

A few minutes later, I said good-bye to my husband and was led into a sterile room where I was told to sit on the metal table and wait for the anesthesiologist. I breathed deeply, preparing myself for the worst part of a c-section: the epidural.

There must be something problematic about my vertebrae because no one seems able to get that epidural in on the first try. With my previous babies, I had squeezed Nate's hand while a stranger repeatedly stuck a needle in my back, but this time, Nate was biding his time in a 1950's-style father's waiting room so this time I squeezed the edge of the cold table. It was not as reassuring. The pain made little spots dance in front of my eyes. When the anesthesiologist told me it was over and that I should lie down on my back, I felt nothing but relief.

For about two minutes.

Two minutes is the maximum time you can lie on your back when you are nine months pregnant before the pain in your hips and the pressure on your internal organs becomes all you can think about.

Ten minutes dragged by. Then fifteen.

A new, more chipper nurse entered the room. She had come to apologize profusely. My doctor was running late, as her mother had fallen that morning and hit her head. It would be a half hour or so before the surgery could start. She was really sorry, but they would keep monitoring me, and I could just rest there, and they'd start as soon as they possibly could. Would I like her to turn on the radio to keep me company? Without waiting for an answer, she flipped the music on and bustled back out of the room.

Dazed, I listened to the end of a Spanish song I didn't recognize and then groaned when a news report came on next. The announcers just wanted to let us know that there had been a brutal murder in our city early that morning. A wife had killed her husband and then herself. She'd used a knife. The report was very detailed. (I briefly wondered if the woman had been pregnant and her husband had suggested she lie on her back. If so, maybe the homicide was justified.)

By this point I was beginning to feel a bit hysterical. Was this the birth of one of my precious children or was I trapped in a badly-written sitcom?

When the reporter finally stopped describing the bloody scene and music began to play again, I took deep breaths to calm myself. Until I recognized the song.

It was Madonna singing "Like a Virgin."

Lying alone on that operating table like a beached whale, I laughed out loud until tears streamed down my face.

Suddenly I knew exactly how I was going to write this up for my friends. And I knew that whoever this baby turned out to be, I would tell them the story of this moment and I would teach them to appreciate the delight of their having been ushered into the world in the company of such perfect irony.

This is one of the best things we can offer each other, this space to laugh when life is no laughing matter. Whenever I sit with a devastated friend and we make jokes about the very situation that's caused them pain, we always say, "This isn't really funny," but we keep laughing anyway. Not because we're callous and indifferent, but because, dang it, we can laugh if we want to. Our laughter is our own small victory.

Is that laughter inappropriate? Definitely. But, honestly, it's the horrible crap that has happened that is really inappropriate. Once the S.S. Appropriate has already sailed; laughing at the mess it left behind isn't going to make it any worse.

Sometimes you can't find the laughter, of course. You can't always summon joy at will. But you can choose the people you keep close. You can choose people who stay, who provide safe places, who listen to the whole truth and keep on listening. And when you're with them, sometimes the laughter will overtake you by surprise.

Our local children's museum has a haunted house every October, and when we first moved back to Indiana, the big kids were the perfect age to enjoy it. They were old enough to want to go and still young enough to find it thrilling. Lucy was only two, and since I am not a fan of haunted houses, I was happy to stay outside with her while Nate took the others inside.

On the day they went, Ellie was giddy with excitement, and Scott gripped Nate's hand with a determined smile.

They were gone for a long time, and when they finally came out the other side, I asked how it had gone. Nate grinned.

"They were pretty scared at some parts," he said, "but Scott was brave, and Ellie..." He pointed to where she was giggling. "Ellie literally never stopped laughing."

Of course she didn't. She's my girl.

What else is there to do when life is too much? When you're terrified, when you're overwhelmed, when you're depressed? You reach out for the people around you. You cry as long as you can, but when your tears run out, you have to get on with life. You have to stand up and walk on through the dark.

So you hold your dad's hand as tightly as you can, you remind yourself that he's never let you down, you look over at your equally terrified little brother, and you giggle your way through to the other side.

Part 4

Laughing at The Dark

21

It's Not the Fall That Kills You, But You Might Wish It Was

Twelve years ago, our friend Mario left his sister's house early in the morning. He hadn't planned to spend the night, but his visit went late the evening before, and it had made more sense to sleep where he was. It was still dark when he began walking to the train that would take him to work. As in many poor neighborhoods on the outskirts of Buenos Aires in those days, there were no streetlights to show his way, but Mario knew where he was going. He had a family, four young sons and a daughter, and he worked hard to provide for all of them. He was no stranger to leaving home before dawn.

He had to cross the street to get to the train station. The driver of the car passing through wasn't using any headlights, probably in a misguided attempt to save money. Without warning, Mario was struck down in the darkness. As far as anyone knows, he died on impact.

After all these years, I can still feel my heart seize up when I think of the phone call that took Nate out to help

Mario's widow and young son identify his body. I can still feel the numbness of the weeks that followed.

Sometimes in this world, just when you've found a way to live and work with the darkness you know, something even darker comes for you. There is no predicting it and there is no avoiding it.

Years after Mario's death, I stood at my computer in my kitchen in a different city in Argentina and opened my email to read words that landed like a punch to my gut. Our teammates, the ones we relied on for work and life and who had only recently gone home for a short, scheduled visit, were now thinking of not returning. They hadn't made a final decision—though it was clear what was going to happen—and while they knew it would change all of our lives, they didn't want to discuss it with any of us. It wasn't a long email, just a few unemotional sentences, but I knew things would never be the same.

I have felt my feet knocked out from under me. I have tumbled helplessly into the valley of night. I have seen friends and family endure the same dizzying fall. In that darkest of all dark places, despair presses in. It feels impossible to resist. It IS impossible to resist.

I don't know of any way to prevent that tumble. When it comes, it comes. It's part of the journey. The only hopeful word I can offer is that in the valley of the shadow, there is more to be found than death.

There's an old Leslie Philips song that says, "There's a river of love that runs through all times." There's a river of grief, the song also says, and a river of tears and of dark fire, but the river of love runs through it all. It runs through the freezing cold and the icy dark. It runs through the searing heat and the driest of deserts. When you are in that valley, the river will feel like it exists only to drown you, but you were made to be buoyed by its irresistible current.

Some people choose to take up residence in the valley of night. They embrace cynicism, having found it futile to climb out on their own. They content themselves with making fleeting sparks that feel good for a moment, believing that's all that really exists.

I know where they're coming from. They aren't wrong about the impossibility of climbing out. The only way out is down and into that wonderful, terrifying river. And while the river of love can carry you out of the valley, there's no way to see where it's rushing you off to.

It's a long, dark journey. A cold journey, and wet.

And who knows exactly what waits for you at the end?

22

Maybe It's Time To Embrace The Suck

A few winters ago, I discovered the existence of something called a polar vortex. As a sci-fi fan, I thought the term sounded thrilling, in a dangerously exciting kind of way. Ha. The reality, while certainly dangerous, is far from exciting.

A sustained cold snap with a windchill of negative 30 brings everything to a halt. School is cancelled, playing outside is off the table, running errands and even driving to work is kept to a minimum. It literally freezes life as you know it.

Except for your children. They are not frozen. They are inside your house, moving constantly.

In our second winter of polar vortex, we had one very rough week. There was no snow or ice on the roads, but temperatures were brutally low. School was called off a couple of days in a row, and by the third day, a couple of my mom friends and I decided we absolutely had to get some social activity for the kids. We set up a play date for early afternoon, and in a fit of inspiration, I decided to drive my kids downtown to have lunch with Nate at work before heading to our friends' house.

The drive wasn't bad. Roads were clear. The car kept us warm. The pizza was delicious. The kids were happy to be out and about.

Our friends lived close to us, so we were back only a mile from home when I came to a stop, left turn signal on, prepared to turn into their driveway. I waited for a few oncoming cars to pass, then made my turn.

Halfway through it, I heard a horrible crash and jerked against my seatbelt. Shattered glass flew everywhere as my SUV spun out of control and into my friend's front yard. We bumped down the embankment and came to a halt. Scott and Lucy were in the backseat crying loudly. I glanced over to the passenger seat where Ellie stared back at me, dry-eyed but pale and tense, then whirled to the back. My babies were there, whole and apparently not bleeding.

"Is everyone okay?"

"What happened? What happened?" they cried.

"Someone hit us, but we're all here. We're all okay. It's going to be okay."

A part of my brain registered that Lucy had broken glass on her lap and in her hair.

It was my window that had smashed, but luckily I could still open my door. Telling the kids to stay put, I climbed out. The whole side of the car was folded in. A pickup truck was sitting on the road, its front end smashed. Tomatoes littered the ground, some on the pavement and some in the snowy grass. The old man who had been driving the truck was gathering them up. He seemed confused about what had happened.

My first priority was to get the kids out and check on them. They climbed out into the frigid wind, each shaking but apparently unharmed. I wrapped them in a hug, only remembering, now that they were safe, that it was twenty below zero. Ellie was weirdly calm as she asked if she should take them inside. Yes, I told her, and tell the other moms what happened.

I went to speak with the other driver, but he just kept babbling about how I came out of nowhere and he couldn't answer any questions. It was clear from the damage on our two cars that he had t-boned me from behind as I made my left turn. Hands shaking, I called 911.

By the time emergency vehicles were on their way, I couldn't feel my hands and feet. My friends came outside, alarmed at what my kids had reported. We waited together for the police and ambulance. When they arrived, the scene took on an even more surreal appearance.

While the EMTs checked out my children inside the house, I described the accident to the police officer. He took notes, and we walked around to see the damage on the car. That was when I first truly saw the point of impact. It was right at the rear edge of the driver's side back door. My little Lucy had been sitting in a booster seat just inside that door. A few inches difference, and she would have been crushed.

Numb from shock and frigid temperatures, something in me distantly felt the horror of that almost-reality. All I could think was that I should never have left home that day.

I don't know if it's biological wiring or cultural expectations, but most of the moms I know inherently believe that if something bad happens, it means they have done something wrong. Your son breaks a dish at someone else's house? You should have been watching him more closely. Your daughter makes another kid cry? You should have taught her better. Your baby is sick? You should have identified the symptoms sooner. You straggle into church late, with only half the required number of shoes on feet? You're a terrible mom who can't get it together.

It's like we think that if we were doing life right, it wouldn't be this difficult.

If that lie doesn't make you laugh, you just haven't lived long enough yet.

If I've learned anything in life so far, it's that you could be Oprah, Beyoncé, and Mother Theresa all rolled into one, and bad stuff would still happen to you.[1] Because this world is a wild place, and you aren't the only person living here.

I'm not always a perfect driver, but that day, I had done everything right. My car was in good condition. The roads were clear. It was broad daylight. We all wore seatbelts. I drove the speed limit and used my turn signal. I was alert and undistracted.

I didn't have to mess up for something horrible to happen.

Sometimes accidents happen and they can't be prevented. Sometimes someone else makes the mistake, and I have to live with the consequences. Sometimes my kids have to live with the consequences.

That day, on that road, it was an accident. That old man had no intention of hurting my children. Another car had turned out, he had gotten confused, and he had swerved when he shouldn't have. We just happened to be in the way.

Hard as we try to prevent it, people hurt us and they hurt our kids. Sometimes it's good people who make mistakes. Sometimes it's bad people who make decisions.

---

[1] Remember Mary, the woman God chose to be the mother of his only son? She lost her kid once and didn't find him for days. Who exactly do we think we are?

Reckless comments from family members about their appearance or abilities. Kids at school who are petty and cruel. Friends who betray them.

Stalkers on the internet. Men who yell vile things at our daughters. Drunk drivers.

Yes, it is our job to live wisely. We wear seatbelts and learn about boundaries and walk away from abusers. We don't touch hot stoves and we don't put our faith in liars.

But no one gets through life unscathed. How would you even do that? And how lonely would it be to try?

As much as our job is to keep our kids alive, it's even more important to teach them how to live, how to navigate dangers, how to ask the right questions.

The question isn't how to prevent others from hurting you. The question is how to live a life of joy in a world where others will sometimes hurt you. Because I know there are some things you can't laugh at, but weirdly, you can still be happy in a world where they exist.

I have not found joy by locking my family in where we can never get hit by a careless driver.

I've found joy by going out into the cold beautiful world. I've found it by marveling at my ten-year-old daughter's ability to be calm in crisis. I've found it by helping the old man who hit me pick up his tomatoes off the roadside. I've found it in my friends bringing me hot tea as I wait in the snow. I've found it in snuggling my five-year-old under a heated blanket and watching Frozen in the pediatric ER while doctors make sure her injured shoulder is okay.[2]

Maybe you'll find joy in a different way than I do. I can't tell you where you'll discover it, but I suspect you will be surprised. I suspect it will be hidden where you never thought to look. It might even be hidden where it doesn't seem to belong.

To steal a quote from the great Tim Riggins,[3] "I think it's time to embrace the suck." Because joy doesn't live somewhere far away from the crap of life, joy lives in the middle of it.

It may be the weirdest truth of this dangerously exciting world.

----

[2] It was.

[3] I am not ashamed of my love of "Friday Night Lights" or of my plan to name my next dog Tim Riggins. I can only hope that Rigsie will live up to his name and be tough and lovable all at the same time.

23

I Have My One Thing...

If I had to list the top five skills of my children as preschoolers, packing would easily make number one. Through some freak of genetics, they inherited their father's instinct for collecting things and my predisposition to be constantly mobile, and they combined these traits into the habit of stuffing every toy they owned into any bag they could find and carrying it all around with them wherever they went.

Sometimes they wouldn't even play with the toys. Just pack and carry. (And leave in an unlikely place so the next time you wanted a particular item it couldn't be found by any logical method.)

When Ellie was four and Scott two, the habit was starting to wear pretty thin for me. Anytime we were trying to leave the house, I'd look over and two little people would be stuffing things into purses, no shoes on, no coat on, no time for hair combing. The bags must be packed!

After a few unsuccessful attempts at reasoning with them, one day I put my foot down.

We were headed to the swing set outside our apartment building, and when Ellie began packing for a two-week vacation, I wasn't having it.

"We don't need to take toys with us," I said. "We're only going outside to play for a while."

"I just need a few little things," she begged. "Please. Just a few little things."

"You may bring one thing," I relented. "Only one. And you are responsible to bring it back inside when we're done."

"Three things, just three things."

"One."

She began to cry. "I really need these two things," she sobbed, holding up two overstuffed purses.

Please note that each purse was filled with a myriad of other items, so I felt that I was being generous when I said, "You may bring one purse."

The tears went on for a few more seconds and then stopped abruptly. Ellie jumped up from the floor. "Mommy, I just need one minute!" she said cheerily and disappeared into her bedroom.

A few seconds later she reappeared with a giant purse, quickly stuffed both smaller purses inside it, then added a few random toys for good measure. "Okay, Mommy!" she said, holding up the bag that was now half her size. "I have my one thing!"

These are the moments they don't warn you about before you have kids. The moments where your kid's cleverness merges with their rebellion and you are torn between pride and despair.

Who is this little schemer that I'm raising, and what am I supposed to do with her?[1]

There's just so much we need our kids to learn, you know? There's so much we hope for them and even more that we fear for them. I want to encourage my daughter's creative problem-solving, but I also want her to accept the rules I lay down for her well-being. I want her to develop her bright mind but I don't want her to be an inconsiderate smartass.

Woven through all the worries about feeding our kids and getting them through school and monitoring how much TV they watch is the central question:

What will become of them? Or, better put, what will they become?

Whether it's the specific genes they've inherited or just the nature of all humans, your kids will be dishonest and lazy and cruel sometimes. They'll be selfish pretty much all the time, especially at first. Meanwhile, the world is trying to force them into a mold. You can see the darker

---

[1] That day I let her take the bag because, in my book, if you're smart enough to find a way around the rules without hurting anyone, you should get the rewards of your wit. Don't you think?

influences on every side. You see the roles they are expected to fill, the boxes they are supposed to confine themselves to.

Sometimes it feels like everything, inside them and outside, is pushing our kids in the wrong direction. I know I'm not the only one lying in bed many nights worrying that they won't push back.

We're all wondering what the secret is to having our kids turn out "right." How do we ensure they make good choices and become good people?

We don't. We can't.

Listen, God is, by definition, the perfect father, and look how many of his children live in rebellion. I don't know why he doesn't just force everyone to be good when he has the power to do that, but for some reason, he doesn't. That's not the world he thought was best.

When I'm not sure what I'm supposed to do as a mom, I remember what Father God does.

First, he loves us deeply, unconditionally, sacrificially. From the moment of our creation, he stamps us with our ultimate identity as his dearly loved children. People who are loved are valuable. That's what value means. The value of something is what someone is willing to pay for it. Eternal God paid his whole self for us. That's how much we're worth.

Second, God was, is, and always will be, himself. The God who makes order out of chaos. The God who creates and nourishes life. The God who brings calamity and then brings redemption. The God of forgiveness. The God of justice. The God who is three in one, living in constant community, unity in diversity. The God who doesn't leave, who keeps his promises, who can handle anything. The God who speaks only truth. He is himself, openly before us, showing us who he is at every turn, offering us what he has. That's who he was before he made us. That's who he'll be when we are dust.

Presented with this kind of love and this kind of example, we experience a choice. Sometimes we make the right one and find abundant life and sometimes we choose to weigh ourselves down with crap.

Our children are no different. Whether they realize it or not, we've already given them their chief identity as people who are loved. They are of immense value because we have loved them, we love them now, and we will love them forever.

All that is left is for us to live our lives as the people we want our children to be.

What do you want for your kids and why do you want it? Be that. Own that. Is your faith the true faith? Then live it. Do you think friendships are important? Cultivate some. Do you value mental health and physical health and strong character? Then pursue those things in your own life.

I'm not saying we don't teach our kids things. Of course we do. I'm not saying we don't impose discipline in their routines. Of course we sometimes have to make them do homework and exercise and music practice that they don't want to do. I'm not saying we don't monitor their emotional and spiritual health and provide people and resources to support those things. That's part of the deal.

But the outcome is out of our hands. Who they become is not up to us. It's up to them and the God who made them.

So, we hope and pray for their future, even as we watch them pack their bags full of things they don't really need, even as we know that they will get tired of carrying all that weight and we'll end up lugging it around for them.

But we're children, too, and our Father has carried our baggage for years, patiently encouraging us to leave it behind but also faithfully bearing it with us until we're ready to listen. So we follow his example. We shoulder what weighs too much and we walk with them all the winding way.

Because it's a lot easier for all of us to find our way when we aren't alone.

24

Shit Happens, and You Just Got Shit On. Sorry.

I think it was the time I accidently dumped a can of beans into the blender while making salsa that I codified the words of my life motto. People were coming to dinner, and there wasn't time to repair the mistake, so I scooped out as many beans as I could, added in the tomatoes that were really supposed to be in there, said to my daughter, "I'm sure it will be fine," and pressed blend.

The reckless confidence of that statement pretty much defines my attitude about most things. Unexplained rash on my child's back? I'm sure it will be fine. Weird noise from the pipes when you flush the toilet? I'm sure it will be fine. Twenty more people coming to the party than what we planned for? I'm sure it will be fine.

Obviously, over the years, I've learned that some rashes and some noises shouldn't be ignored. Even then, though, in the end, things really are usually fine. Most of the time, assuming that things will turn out okay hurts no one and saves a ton of drama.

Every once in a while, though...every once in a while, things are really truly not fine.

A few years ago, on an early spring day, Scott was getting ready for school when he told me he felt sick to his stomach. In our house, fever or vomiting will automatically get you out of school. For all other unverifiable pains and discomfort, each kid has one day per semester to stay home with no protest. The rest of the time, we buck up and make it work. On this particular day, Scott and I agreed that he should go to school and see how he felt as the day went on.

He didn't even make it to 8:00. From what I gather, he got off the bus, walked to his third grade classroom, and immediately hurled in the trash can right inside the door.

I got a call from the nurse. I picked him up. We bought Gatorade on the way home. Bring on the stomach flu.

He threw up every couple of hours all day, but we kept him hydrated and by the end of the day, the vomiting had ended. Unfortunately, though, the diarrhea had begun.

It had been a few years since we'd had such a terrible flu. I took his temperature often, but he didn't have a fever. Still, the diarrhea went on and on. By day three, I was getting worried. I'm not quick to go to the doctor, but I considered it. I even prayed about it. But in the end, I knew there was nothing anyone could do for the flu, and he was still drinking a lot of fluids, so I didn't think there was danger of dehydration.

It seemed like I had made the right choice when he came out of his bedroom that evening and asked for some soup. It was the first food he had wanted in a couple of days, and he ate a whole bowl, along with a couple of crackers while we watched some family TV. My relief was evidence of how thin my confidence had become.

Then suddenly, Scott sat up in the middle of the show and grabbed his belly. "My stomach hurts!" he said through gritted teeth. "It hurts so bad!"

Nate and I looked at each other. We might not be the most of anxious of parents, but we have heard of appendicitis.

"Go," Nate said.

I grabbed my purse, wrapped Scott in a blanket, and we were off to the ER.

One of the beautiful things I had never before appreciated about where I live is that we are only a five-minute drive from a world class children's hospital with its own pediatric emergency room. My boy was not thrilled to be going there at 7:30 at night, but at least it was someplace kid-friendly and close to home.

"It's probably nothing," I told Scott. "You're probably fine and they'll send us back home after they've checked you out. But a stomach pain like this is something you always have to take seriously because there's a small chance it could be a very serious problem."

When we checked in and I gave them his symptoms, no one seemed overly alarmed. They did find us a room, though, and after a bit a doctor came in. She did her initial examination, asking about the location and level of his pain, and her initial diagnosis was that it didn't seem like appendicitis and was most likely just distress from his bout with the flu. Just to be sure, though, they'd give him an x-ray to see what things looked like.

So began the longest night of my life. The x-ray took two hours and then wasn't conclusive, so they decided to order an ultrasound. We were taken to the basement around midnight, where we waited alone in the empty hallway for another hour. Scott was exhausted and sure that there was no good reason to be there. He asked to go home at least fourteen times. Finally, an ultrasound tech came and exacerbated his pain by pressing a wand into his belly for a long time. We were taken back upstairs. At two in the morning, we were told the ultrasound didn't get a good picture and that they'd like to do a CT scan. By this time, another doctor was on duty, and he also was pretty sure it was going to turn out to just be inflammation with no appendix trouble, but they hadn't been able to rule it out yet. I was too tired to do anything but go along. For the CT scan, Scott had to drink a giant cup of liquid, which made him vomit, but eventually we got it down. We had the scan. We waited two more hours. Neither of us slept. At about 5:30, the doctor came back.

The CT scan showed that his appendix *was* inflamed. In fact, it was perforated, and they needed to operate as soon as possible. A surgeon had been paged and was on his way to the hospital.

I texted Nate, who was home with the girls. In minutes, he had called his mom to come stay with them and was on his way to the hospital. He arrived just in time for the lady who comes to explain all the risks of surgery. I think she was a nurse practitioner. I'm honestly not sure. All I know is that I sat there, bleary-eyed from lack of sleep, as she told us that our son's appendix had been leaking bile into the rest of his organs, that his intestines were very inflamed, that there was a risk that they'd have to remove parts of those, too. She talked about what could go wrong with the surgery and what they would do if that happened. She mentioned feeding tubes and infections and drainage ports and the distant possibility of septic shock or even death. She told us to expect a minimum of five days' recovery time in the hospital. She asked if we understood. She asked us to sign the forms.

We signed. I couldn't honestly say that I fully understood.

All of this happened in the room where my nine-year-old was lying. He was dozing in and out, but I didn't know how much he was listening. I'd already told him he needed surgery and held his hand while he cried that he didn't want it. I wasn't about to break down in front of him. It was my job to smile when he opened his eyes. To smile and to say, "It's going to be fine."

It wasn't until I was in the waiting room a little later, where my own parents sat with the breakfast they had brought me, that my tears came in force.

We all waited together during the surgery. Mercifully, it was done quickly and with complete success. The part of my brain that had refused to acknowledge any other outcome was triumphant. I soon learned not to be too hasty.

For the next eight days, I sat in a hospital room, watching my boy slowly, slowly regain the ability to drink and to eat. On the sixth day, when he was cleared for solid food, he eagerly ordered a cheeseburger and found that he couldn't eat more than two bites. On the eighth day, they allowed us to take him home, but two days later, his fever spiked. He cried when I took him back to the hospital.

He had an infection. Luckily, installing the drainage tube and pic line was an outpatient procedure, so we were only there for the day. I learned how to inject antibiotics and how to clean the ports. We got to be at home, but we had to report back once a week for a blood draw and change of bandages. Each time, my son sat in one of those chairs where cancer patients sit for chemo treatment. He looked so weak and scared in that chair, but I breathed deep and thanked God we weren't there for anything more serious.

The day his pic line came out, we got ice cream. The day he went back to school, we celebrated with cheeseburgers he could actually eat. And when he finally joined his baseball team on the field for their last game of the season, I played it cool when he was looking and cried quietly when he wasn't.

It was over. It would be several months before he regained his full strength, but he was okay. We had come out of the long tunnel, and once again I was sure things would be fine.

But by then, I had altered my definition of fine. It no longer meant things wouldn't go badly. It only meant that we would deal with whatever happened.

On the second day of our hospital stay, when my son was still sleeping all the time and unable to have any liquid by mouth even when he cried from thirst, a new nurse came on duty. She had been working the inpatient floor of the children's hospital for ten years, and I couldn't even imagine all the things she had seen. When she finished taking his vitals that first time, she paused for a few minutes to talk. She told stories of how difficult appendicitis can be to diagnose, and I realized that she didn't want me to blame myself for what had happened. She repeated more than once that there was no way I could have known.

"Forgive my language," she said, "but shit happens, and you just got shit on. I'm sorry."

My first thought was that I was definitely going to embroider that on a pillow. My second thought was pure gratitude that this woman had been assigned to our room that day.

Forgive my language, but shit happens. Shit happens to children as well as to adults, no matter how much we feel like it shouldn't. The children's hospital is proof enough of that.

My son suffered pretty severely, but at least it was of relatively short duration. At least he would eventually return to normal. Some of the kids on our floor would not. One day, a baby down the hall cried nonstop for hours. The rooms were very private, but on a trip to the ice machine, I heard talk of severe burns. Several times during our stay, a wagon was pulled past our open door. The child riding in it had a bald head.

Kids suffer. They experience pain. Sometimes, for all our hard work and medical knowledge, there is nothing we can do to stop it. We can only help them bear it.

For us it was quiet company and not a lot of hovering and questions. It was ice cream and Legos and Minecraft Story Mode. It was scientific discussions of the brain's reaction to stress and pain, which distracted him from the actual stress and pain. It was trivia games and hands to squeeze and the same calm answers to the same frustrated questions over and over.

Because Scott missed so much school, his third-grade class made him get well cards that his teacher delivered in person. Our favorite was the card from a little girl who is still one of Scott's good friends. In big block letters it said, "Sorry your appendix tried to kill you!"

That blunt and cheerful expression of sympathy seems like a small and silly thing to make a difference in a dark time, but it was exactly what we needed. We still refer to that spring as the time Scott's appendix tried to kill him. We laugh when we say it, but not without a little shiver.

Scott doesn't really like to talk about those days. I don't blame him. Remembering brings up all the emotions for me, too. But spoken or unspoken, it's a part of his story. A story being written by someone who is not like us, with an ending we can't see yet.

We're several years down the road now, and my boy has turned into a teenager with a lot of grit. Maybe it's in the DNA —his father is as determined as they come—and maybe he would have been this way no matter what. But I can't help thinking that those days of experiencing pain, both physical and emotional, taught him something about what he can endure.

Or maybe I'm wrong. Maybe I'm inventing the meaning I want to see. I do believe everything happens for a reason, but I don't believe we always get to know what it is. Maybe this is just a thing that happened to us once, and its purpose had nothing to do with us at all.

Sometimes I think about all the people who were in some way affected by Scott's sickness. The doctors and nurses. Our parents and our daughters and the rest of our family. Scott's classmates and friends. The members of our community who brought us food and Legos. The friends of friends, people we've never met, who prayed for us. The kids on his baseball team that got more time on the field because they were down a player. The acquaintances who heard our story and were quick to recognize the symptoms of appendicitis when it happened to their own children. The complex network of people, each life important, each full of endlessly moving pieces.

I think of the God who loves each of us and who is creating a mind-bendingly intricate masterpiece as he weaves us all together. I'm pretty sure the answer to the question "why?" is "it's complicated."

I'm pretty sure something incredible is happening all around us, but we're too small to see it from the angle that would make sense of it all.

All we can see is that shit happens, and life moves on.

Left with no option, we adjust our definitions of fine and we move on with it.

25

We Just Can't Live With A Terrified Chipmunk

Before his emergency appendectomy, Scott's only experience with a hospital had been his birth in a lovely private one in Buenos Aires, Argentina.

The decision to have him there was easy. We had lived nearby for four years. His sister's stubborn refusal to be born had caused an emergency c-section and meant that Scott could be born on a schedule. We would know the exact day of his birth weeks in advance and could plan for my parents to visit and help take care of things at home.

I also loved my Argentine doctor. He was a slightly older George Clooney type who had taken great care of me through two pregnancies, even if he did mention my weight gain a few too many times.[1]

---

[1] I kid you not, after Scott's c-section, Dr. Larosa casually told me that while he was in there he liposuctioned out a little of the fat around my incision area.. You know, so I could get back to a bikini sooner rather than later.

We were excited for our son to be fully Argentine (not to mention how his citizenship would help us end our years-long paperwork process and achieve the coveted status of permanent resident).[2] I'd been through a c-section before, I'd asked lots of questions about what differences to expect in a new country, and I felt ready for a cross-cultural birth.

If only I had known all the right questions to ask.

In many ways the experience was better. I would never have chosen this route, but the truth is that scheduled c-sections are a dream. I got up and took a shower. I kissed my daughter and my mother good-bye. We drove calmly to the hospital and checked in. When Ellie was born, I spent a long sleepless night of induction, then endured horrible hours of pitocin-induced contractions only to end up in an emergency c-section featuring way too much anesthesia which caused horrible tremors and nausea. With Scott, we had a few bad moments while they put in the epidural and then a quick and painless delivery with no anesthesia side-effects at all. Instead of Ellie's smashed nose that had to be taped in place, Scott had the perfectly smooth, round face of a much older baby.[3]

Physically speaking, it was ideal.

---

[2] Yes, I had an anchor baby. Make of that what you will.

[3] He was also a whopping nine pounds. Thank you, c-section.

Emotionally, though, I kept getting spun in circles. Here's a little life tip: If you decide to have a major milestone experience in a foreign country, be prepared for lots of fun surprises along the way. I mean, you should totally do it. Just know that there are going to be moments when you feel...stupid. That's really the only word for it.

My first chance to feel like an idiot came shortly after our arrival that morning. Someone had warned me that the hospital wouldn't provide diapers or blankets or anything for the baby, so we had come prepared for that, but when the nurse asked if I had brought supplies for my own recovery, I had a moment of panic. It had never occurred to me that I would need that. This was a hospital, right? In the US, you arrive with an extra pair of sweatpants in an overnight bag and they take it all from there.

In Argentina, the nurse sighed as I told her that I did not in fact have all the necessary pads and girdles already purchased. Also, girdle? I needed a girdle? What are you even talking about?[4]

She gave me the look you give to a flighty, thoughtless young thing when you are trying to be patient with her. She told Nate there was a pharmacy across the street and

---

[4] The answer was a wide band to help hold my wobbly stomach in place so my incision would be supported. It was the most genius solution to c-section recovery I could have imagined, and I cursed my doctors in the U.S. for not suggesting one. Having a c-section? Get yourself a girdle, friend. You won't be sorry.

gave him a list of what was needed. I waited around feeling foolish while he went to have an extremely awkward conversation with a pharmacist.

After the surgery and our first glorious meeting with our son, we found ourselves alone with our baby and a whole long afternoon before the brief visiting hours in the evening. We were fine, but it was an emotional letdown.

On Ellie's birth day, the hospital was packed with friends and family eagerly waiting for her. She didn't come until late at night, and I have photos of a crowd of people peeking in the nursery window to get a first glimpse of her. After they all went home for the night, I held my daughter, and then the nurses gently suggested that they take her for a while to let me sleep. I gratefully agreed. From then on, any moment that I wasn't feeding the baby or sleeping, we had visitors or nurses buzzing around offering help.

When Scott was born, most of our people were far away, and those that were close were only allowed in during the evening visiting hours. Other than my parents and daughter and one friend, we didn't see anyone that first day. We didn't see much of the nurses, either. The baby was healthy, alert, and quiet, and they pretty much left us to enjoy him. It felt anticlimactic, but I dealt with the emotions pretty well until night fell.

It got dark about the same time the anesthesia wore off, and the painkillers they gave me weren't strong enough. I was hurting. Nate was trying to get comfortable on a reclining chair, which was all he had to sleep on that night. And then the baby started to cry.

After trying to soothe him for a while without causing myself more pain, I asked Nate to call the nurse. I had already asked for more medicine and knew I wasn't going to get it, but I figured if the baby could go to the nursery for a while, I could try to get some rest at least.

He pressed the call button. After a few moments the nurse arrived.

"The baby is a little fussy, and I'm feeling exhausted," I said, remembering all those nurses anxious to help me rest up from my last birth.

She looked at me sympathetically and waited for more.

"He just doesn't seem to want to sleep, and I need some rest," I explained.

"Would you like me to bring you a bottle to give him?" she asked.

I was confused. "No, I already nursed him. He's just awake and I need to sleep for a bit."

It was her turn to be confused. Nate was holding the baby.

"Could you maybe just take him for a little bit?" I asked more directly.

She shook her head. "I'm not allowed to do that unless there's something medically wrong."

Nate and I looked at each other as the truth began to dawn. This hospital had no nursery. This baby was not going to leave our room.

After an awkward pause, the nurse said that if we didn't need anything she had to go. We nodded tiredly. She left.

In retrospect, it makes perfect sense. No Argentine would ever voluntarily send their baby to be watched by strangers during his first few nights on earth. You keep your kids with you. It's just how it works.

At the time, though, tired and in pain and already feeling lonely, I experienced a moment of despair. My sweet baby who had been quiet and sleepy all day was clearly now going to be loud and awake all night.

And we were on our own.

Maybe you've had this moment. The moment when you look around for someone to rescue you and realize that no one is coming. You're the adult. You're the one who has to do the rescuing.

That day in September was my first time. It wouldn't be the last. I'd pretty much spend the next decade having moments like that. Even now the only thing that's different is that I know better than to waste time looking around for a miracle.

I talk about community constantly. I've dedicated my life to building community. I live rooted in community. But sometimes, in some moments, being an adult is lonely business. It's just you and the task ahead, and there's no one who can climb that mountain (or molehill) for you.

Just last week, I came home from taking Lucy for a flu shot in time to hear Ellie scream. "I saw something small and furry run into Lucy's room!"

Lucy, on an entirely different level of our house, immediately jumped onto a chair and refused to come down. Ellie shut herself in her room.

And me? I did the very last thing I wanted to do. I went into Lucy's room and systematically searched every corner, until I did, in fact, find a chipmunk hiding behind her desk.

So, here's the story: A couple of years ago, my father-in-law rescued a litter of kittens that had been abandoned in one of his work trucks. My mother-in-law nursed them for weeks, often inviting my children over to play with them and encouraging them to name the kitties, like the evil genius that she is.

Obviously, when they were old enough to eat solid food, my children begged me to take one of them home. Nate voted against it but left it up to me. That kitten was just so dang cute. And my girls wanted him so badly.

Long story short, we brought Oliver Queen home, quickly shortened his name to Ollie, and he's been with us ever since. Ollie is the friendliest cat with the the loudest purr I've ever heard. He is a love. He is also dedicated to his feral roots, and loves to roam outside hunting small furry animals, which he then brings inside as a gift to his beloved family.

It was bad enough when they were dead, but at some point he started bringing them in alive to play with them first. Do you have any idea how much mess is created when an injured bird flutters around your dining room for a while before being killed by a cat?

Sorry for that image. My point is that bloody feathers are awful to clean up.

My other point is that chipmunks are really good at hiding and run very fast when you try to catch them and ~~throw them~~ gently place them outside.

A couple of months ago, I asked Ellie to hold the bucket for me while I nudged a live chipmunk out of the pantry and into the waiting receptacle. As planned, it darted out of the pantry, but it bypassed the bucket completely. It headed straight for Ellie, who jumped back and landed ON THE CHIPMUNK, resulting in one dead chipmunk and one twisted ankle.

Yes, that really happened.

Which is why Ellie handled last week's chipmunk by closing her bedroom door firmly. I didn't blame her. I wanted to do the same thing.

But I'm the grown-up. So whatever I may be feeling, it's my job to get the terrified chipmunk out of the house. Because we just can't live with a terrified chipmunk.[5]

When a thing has to be done, the grownup does it. That's what makes you a grownup. Literally nothing else. No special powers. No special bag of tools. No special knowledge.

There's no guidebook for this. There's just doing what has to be done. Anyone who says otherwise is selling something.

People keep asking me if I regret my decision to adopt Ollie. In all honestly, sometimes I do. I could have happily lived my whole life without knowing what a rabbit's scream sounds like. But the regret is always temporary. The truth is that Ollie is wonderful, and when he purrs, the whole world seems right.

Anyway, his value to me isn't defined by a list of pros and cons. There's no spreadsheet that can tally whether the joy he brings outweighs the stress. How I feel about that depends on the day. But I love him. That's his value, not in how much he loves us, but in how much we love him

---

[5] It took about an hour of chasing the chipmunk around the house with a broom, a delighted cat, a very worked up dog, two hours of patiently waiting for it to come out of the hole it found to hide in, and then a quick sweep out the front door, but I'm happy to report that it made it back into the wild alive. This time.

and in the good it does us to love something unconditionally.

Obviously, my love for my cat doesn't even compare to my love for my kids or my husband or my friends or my friends' kids. The sacrifices I'm willing to make aren't even on the same planet. But the principle is the same. Every time I make the choice to love someone, it's a choice to throw away the list of pros and cons. It's a choice to step up, even if I have no clue what I'm doing and it feels like I'm doing it alone.

I have no memory of how we survived that first night with Scott. When you look for rescue and it doesn't come, you just do the best you can. When you've been cut open and sewn back together, and somehow it's someone else who is crying, you grit your teeth through the pain and you take care of them.

I don't know how we did it, but I know that we did. And I know that we have been profoundly changed by stepping up that night and all the nights after.

Welcome to the Twenty-First Century. We're the grownups now.

And surprise! Being a grownup is awesome. Not because of what you receive. Not because of what you achieve. But because of who you get to be. You get to be brave. You get to be honest. You get to be thoughtful and hardworking and loyal. You get to be the person you want to be.

You get to love and love and love, to do hard things, and to pour yourself out for others. And there is no joy in all the world that is greater than the joy of loving like that.

26

Slightly Better Than Total Despair

A while back, a good friend dropped by late at night to vent. Sometimes life just feels impossible, and if you can't rage to the people who love you, where is the rage supposed to go? We poured a glass of wine, and she let loose for a long time. The details aren't important. As we all know, many people are miserable and a few of them feel it's their life's duty to make things miserable for everyone else, too. Suffice it to say, she had encountered some of those people.

We joined in her anger, sympathized with her pain, cracked a few dark jokes, and finally I said, "Well, at least you can always come yell at our house."

"Yeah," she said, "you're slightly better than total despair."

When I was done laughing, I told her that was going to be the name of my autobiography. (Hopefully this one chapter will be enough.) Of all my accomplishments, this one I can claim with the most confidence. I am slightly better than total despair.

Despair is a feeling I did not understand for most of my life.

Don't get me wrong. When I was young, I knew the world was a mess. Before I ever married or was remotely ready to be a mom, I thought long and hard about the wounded cry of my generation, "How can it be right to bring children into such a horrible world?" I felt the pull of that logic—it's pretty hard to argue with—but ultimately I rejected it. If no one walking in the light brings children of light into the world, then we've just resigned ourselves that the darkness will win. At the time, that level of surrender eluded me.

Even now, I believe in the decision to hope. I stand by my choice to have three children, and I still see them as brightly burning flames in the darkness. But in my long-ago idealism, I never could have imagined the terror of watching the dark wind beat against those flames, of seeing the shadows dance around them and not knowing how it all will play out. When I chose this path, I had not yet experienced the gut punch of pouring my whole self into something only to fail and then fail again. I did not yet believe that real people I trusted with my life would turn out to be liars or that their lies could be so pervasive and persistent.

I knew the world was dark, but I didn't know that the darkness would come at me in such deep and personal ways, or that I would feel so helpless when it did.

Several years ago, my friend called me on the phone at 3:15 on a November afternoon. I know the exact time because I was waiting for my kids to get off the school bus at any moment. She was calling to ask me to come pick up her children. She had just found out that her husband was a fraud and that they had no money or jobs. She was trying to find him. She was trying to find the truth. She was trying to hold it together, and it was too soon for the kids to know anything was wrong.

I picked up my kids and then picked up hers. We had after school snacks and played games, and I put on a movie when my husband called. He was dry-heaving on the phone. He had just spent the last several hours talking to the friend in question. It was worse than we had imagined.

Sick to my stomach, I drove my sweet friend's children home at bedtime. I held her two-month-old baby as she put the older kids to bed. Pacing the living room, I bounced that tiny infant and prayed without words. It was the first of many hundreds of moments where I offered an extra pair of hands as she miraculously mothered her children through one of the most hellish experiences anyone can face.

My friend's story is her story, and it's not my place to tell it here. I will only say this: I know now that the things I fear, the things I think I cannot survive, I can. And whatever I think I couldn't stand for my children to bear, God help me—God help us all—we can.

If you are reading this right now with a spirit that is crushed from loving your sweet children through suffering you never wanted for them, my whole heart is with you. I know their pain is what threatens to break you. When you're clinging to the last broken beam from the shipwreck of your dreams, the sick fear that your tiny passengers will drown can almost pull you under.

I know it feels like you can't hold on long enough to get them through.

Just hold on a little longer, okay?

In that dark sea, maybe you can't look high enough to find hope. But maybe for now, you can raise your eyes just the smallest bit, can find something slightly better than total despair.

There are so many of us here if you need us.[1]

---

[1] I wish I could come over to each one of your houses, could make you a cup of tea, could listen to your story until the wee hours of the morning. In the next life, I hope. But there is an email address in my bio at the end of this book. If you write to me, I will read your words and I will do my best to answer. It's not much. But it's slightly better than total despair.

27

I May Ask God To Smite You, But At Least I'll Leave It To Him

I have never thought of myself as an angry person. Yes, I have flaming red hair, and yes, everyone always assumes I must have an equally fiery temper, but really I don't. I'm even-tempered and happy. Intense? Yes. Strong-willed? Yes, okay, that too. But not angry. At least I never used to be.

Nate always had the corner on that particular emotion.[1] When we were first married, I looked over at him once while he was driving and saw him flexing his fingers into a claw shape.

"What are you doing?" I asked.

---

[1] Enneagram 8 if you care about such things.

"I'm imagining that I'm throwing lightning at those drivers," he said. "It's very satisfying."

I laughed. I may not have carried a ton of anger around, but the vicious instinct still made sense to me.

After that, I'd often see him flick his hand in a similar gesture. I knew it meant he was in full Sith mode, and that whoever he was looking at was in mortal danger from force lightening. It was like a little window into his state of mind. Uh-oh, lightning fingers. Time to politely say good-bye to this person.

Imaginary lightning is brilliant, really. Anger has to have somewhere to go or it eats you up. Some people scream and yell. Some people punch walls. Some people punch people, which is really not recommended. When you think about it, briefly fantasizing about frying someone isn't the worst way to cope.

A few years later, though, on the south side of Buenos Aires, I saw what happened when lightning fingers weren't enough. When we moved into our janky apartment in the neighborhood where we worked, our neighbors and friends were wonderful. They helped us fix the place up, they recommended solutions to our many logistical problems, they stopped by to drink *mate* and chat. We wanted our home to be welcoming and open, so even though we lived in a place where everyone had bars on their windows and locked doors at all times, we made a couple copies of our house key and gave them to some of the older teens who used our house as a safe place to hang out.

Every one of those kids was extremely respectful of the trust we had put in them. But one day they came to us and told us that some guys in a neighborhood gang had threatened them, telling them they'd beat them up if they didn't hand over the key to our house. At the time, Nate and I made a salary that was well below the poverty line in the United States, but in our neighborhood, the steady income in US dollars meant we were rich. We had a computer in our apartment. And a PlayStation. We were prime targets for robbery.

To protect our friends, we took back all the keys. If they didn't have access, they couldn't be threatened on our account. We changed the lock on the front door and went on with our lives. The kids never got beat up for telling us, and we never got robbed.

But the anger we felt lingered. At its core, it was a righteous anger. Someone took a loving act of friendship and used it against us. We made a step toward having all things in common, and they took that away, causing pain to the very people we were trying to love. Like all righteous anger, though, ours bled easily into unrighteous anger. How dare they threaten us? How dare they make us look foolish for being generous? Didn't they know what we could do to them if we wanted?

For me, the anger simmered slowly down into deep sadness. For Nate, it burned like banked coals. During the weeks that followed, he would have regular outbursts at other drivers on the road or people in line at the grocery store. The rage was always right there under the surface, within easy reach. Nothing I said helped.[2] When it became clear that it was getting worse and not better, I told him he had to start talking to someone: our mentors, our teammates, a friend. Like the wise man he is, he did just that, and slowly the anger found places to be released.

It may sound weird, but the direction we took our anger most often was toward God. All my life I had been told to take my troubles and place them at the feet of Jesus. That year, I learned that it's also okay to throw them in his face sometimes. Yes, really. It turns out that the God of the universe is quite tough and can take a beating when the children he loves really need to dish one out.

He will also listen while we curse other people. I'm not making this up; it's in the Bible. Have you ever read those Psalms where David says things to God like, "Strike all my enemies on the jaw; break the teeth of the wicked"?[3] Those are called imprecatory psalms, poems that call down disaster on people that deserve it. They're vicious and they're graphic and they're incredibly helpful.

---

[2] Sometimes you can provide perspective for your spouse, but sometimes it's just not possible. At the end of the day, you are one flesh, one person, and what one of you is going through, you both are going through. Sometimes you need someone to counsel you who isn't...you.

[3] Psalm 3:7, and I found that by just opening Psalms and taking the first thing I saw. The Psalms are literally packed with these kinds of prayers.

For the first time, after we had taken back all our keys, I prayed an imprecatory prayer with Nate. Yes, we asked God for protection for our friends and for ourselves. Yes, we asked for wisdom about how to live at peace in a place of turmoil. But then we also asked for God to bring ruin on the men who had tried to bring ruin on us. Destroy them, God. Bring them low. Break their teeth. It's what they have coming.

If that seems unloving to you, I understand, but I believe love is much bigger and more complex than we give it credit for. Love encompasses kindness and compassion and forgiveness, certainly, but it also encompasses truth and exposure and the expectation of right behavior. In an unjust world, love for the oppressed and victimized has to mean justice for the oppressor and perpetrator.

The question is whose job it is to bring about that kind of justice. Though sometimes I'd like to try, I'm not smart enough or powerful enough for the job. So I ask the only person who is. I ask God to make things right, truly right, and because he's my father, I'm free to be totally honest about how I'd like him to do it. Just as I let my kids pour out their wild emotions to me, I throw all my anger toward the person I know can take it. It's okay. I trust him to hear and understand and love me and ignore my advice when it's bad.

I take my need for justice to the appropriate place and then leave it there.[4] Knowing that they deserve it, I ask God to break my enemies' teeth, but I don't go break them myself. I'm not letting my enemies off the hook. I'm freeing myself from the burden of doing God's job.

Hard as it was at the time, I'm glad I learned about imprecatory prayers so early in my adult life. I had no idea how much I was going to need a place for my anger as I got older.

In the last several years, I've been a witness to the devastating mistreatment of many wonderful women I know. Some of my dearest friends, people I've known since we were all young and single and full of hope, have been victims of abuse, of betrayal, of deception, all perpetrated by the men they trusted the most. The domestic abuse that I once thought rare, I now know is happening at alarming rates. It's like there's this curtain, and once you've lifted a tiny corner and peeked behind it, it opens wider and wider, revealing more than you ever thought you'd see.

---

[4] To be clear, part of taking things to God and leaving them in his hands is taking them to the authorities he's instituted. This includes government authorities, church authorities, and family authorities (namely parents). There are people and systems God has put in place to carry out justice on earth. They are imperfect and often fail us, which is why we ultimately trust God and not them, but they are there for our protection however far they can go.

In each of those situations, my first thought and primary energy is to find freedom for the victims and care for their needs. In my experience, that can be stressful and exhausting and overwhelming and depressing, but it is ultimately a privilege, a beautiful and hopeful burden to bear.

The uglier burden is the burden of anger.

You know in the movies or on TV, when the sassy best friend gets to tell off the worthless boyfriend for mistreating the main character? It's my favorite part of any rom-com, especially if she publicly humiliates him in some epic way. In my experience, though, life doesn't work like that. The strong and amazing women I know have stood up to their abusers and done what needed to be done. The good men in my life have stepped up when needed and had direct confrontations with the abusers to reinforce the boundaries that have been set.

My job always lies elsewhere. It lies where it needs to be, with the people who are making their new and hopeful life. It has never fallen to me to look someone in the eyes and tell them exactly how black their soul is. No matter how badly I want to paint their true name on the side of their house or key their car or throw a glass of wine in their face, it has never seemed wise or productive. In fact, I am keenly aware that those actions would only make life worse for the very people I want to help.

Being mature is the worst.

In my heart, a deep and destructive anger burns towards those who have devastated people I love. I have a very active imagination, and you would not like to know the ways I've put it to use in inventing appropriate punishments.

What am I supposed to do with my anger? I don't want it to freeze up inside me, turning my heart bitter and cold. I certainly don't want it to boil over and scald my kids or other innocent people who might be in the wrong place at the wrong time.

It has to go to the only place it can do any good. I lay in bed next to my husband at night and I spit the words out. "God, rain destruction on this evil person. A house fire would be a really nice choice."[5]

So far, no one's house has burned down and no lightning has sprung out to consume anyone, so I guess God has a different plan for justice. But my sweet friends have found freedom and joy and thriving life. I have found freedom and joy and thriving life. Right in the middle of it all being crazy hard.

I suppose that's true justice in the end.

---

[5] I'll never burn anyone's house down, I swear, but if I'm honest, I *would* wish it on my worst enemy. Some people need an apocalypse to have any shot at redemption. So really, it's not unloving at all for me to wish that on them. Sometimes losing everything is the best thing that can happen to you.

28

I Got Nothing

When Ellie was born, home was a second-story apartment in a slum near Buenos Aires. I already wrote about the little bedroom oasis I made for her. The rest of our house, though...let's just say it wasn't exactly baby-proof.

We had worked at it. Though the stairs from the front door originally came up through a giant, unprotected hole in the floor of our living room, we had installed a rail and gate so that no one could fall down. Though the water heater in our shower was originally a small device that you plugged in right there in the shower, we had swapped it out for a gas water heater that ran to the whole house and was less likely to electrocute us.

The one thing we didn't invest in was the back patio. The building where we lived was a big cinderblock cube. The first floor held a storefront which used to be a vegetable shop but was now empty. The second floor was our apartment, which had a back door leading out to a small walled-in cement patio. On the patio were open stairs leading up to the flat roof of the building. It was fun to go up on that roof. You had a view of the neighborhood, and it was a great place to set off fireworks on New Year's

Eve. But those cement stairs had no rails and that roof had no ledge. It was just a flat expanse, two stories above the pot-holed pavement.

When Ellie was a baby, it didn't matter much that those stairs were back there, but when she turned one on the first day of Argentine spring and took her first steps, I diligently built a barrier to block them off. I tacked up a roll of plastic fencing and double-secured it with some Rubbermaid tubs and other patio paraphernalia. It wasn't the classiest thing in the world, but it would keep a child away from the steps, and after all, my extroverted daughter never wanted to be alone, so I'd be with her at all times.

Except, obviously, she was a toddler. So any definitive statement is automatically untrue.

One day about six months later, now in the early stages of pregnancy again and trying desperately to still maintain my house, I had just finished putting away some laundry when I realized Ellie was no longer playing in her bedroom. I called for her and she didn't answer. I wandered from room to room calling her name. Nothing.

I wasn't too worried. It had been less than a minute since the last time I saw her, and our house was totally enclosed. I went into the kitchen, expecting to see her looking for snacks. She wasn't there.

But the back door was open.

That summer we had put a little pool on the patio, and it was her favorite place to be. We spent long hours out there, trying to stay cool in a world without air conditioning. The kitchen door that led onto the patio was always closed when we weren't out there. Apparently, she had learned how to open it. Still, I knew I had drained the pool, so I wasn't panicking until I heard her voice.

"Moooommmmyyyy!"

She didn't sound upset. If anything, that was a happy call. But why did she sound so far away?

I stepped out onto the patio, and my heart stopped.

There was Ellie, less than two years old, looking down at me from the roof. Somehow, in under a minute, she had wormed her way through the barrier, climbed the open staircase and was now standing two stories up with nothing to stop her from falling, if lucky, down one story onto our cement patio, and if not, all the way to the street below.

"Mommy! Look! Mommy! Look!"

She was so proud of herself.

I couldn't risk yelling. If I scared her and she ran toward me, she would fall. I tried to keep my voice cheerful.

"Hey baby, stay right there, okay! Just stay right where you are, and I'll come to you!"

The barrier was much more effective at keeping me out than it had been for her. Still, I tore it apart and raced up the stairs. On the roof, Ellie had more or less obeyed and was standing with a grin, admiring the view.

Picking her up and holding her close had never felt so good.

I carried her down the stairs. I built a new and much better barrier. I spent a lot of time teaching her not to go that way again. I thanked God a million times that it didn't end in the tragedy it could have.

Until we moved out of that neighborhood, I told no one but my husband what had happened. How would two sets of grandparents ever sleep at night if I did? After all, we kept living in that house, swimming in that pool on that patio, walking those dangerous streets.

I knew as well as anyone that sometimes the story is just a near-miss, but sometimes, it's so much more.

A year later, our front doorbell rang, and our sweet co-worker was there in tears. She had just come from the home of a family we worked with in the neighborhood. Their eighteen-month-old baby had drowned in a bucket of water.

There are no words.

The next few days unfolded in horror. The family was devastated, penniless, and had no support system at all. Their oldest daughter, just turned thirteen, had been bringing all her younger siblings, including the baby, to our kids' club for a few years, so they asked Nate to perform the funeral service. With no embalming, everything happens fast, and all day more questions kept coming up, more details coming to light. The bucket was in their back yard. There were multiple adults at home when it happened. Who was supposed to be watching the baby? Were drugs involved? Who left the bucket out? Who was to blame?

As parents, our first responsibility is to keep our kids safe, to keep them healthy, to keep them alive. But the horrible truth is that sometimes we can't. Sometimes we don't. The world, the real world, is unpredictable and beyond our control. It contains things like venomous spiders and cancer and drunk drivers, like flat-topped roofs and buckets of water.

Should someone have dumped out that bucket? Should someone have watched the baby more closely? Yes. Maybe. I don't know. Should I have watched my baby more closely? Should I have built a better barrier to my stairs or refused to live in such an unsafe place? Yes. Maybe. I don't know.

I only know that a thousand near-accidents happen every day. I know that some things can't be predicted and can't be controlled.

My baby didn't fall. Theirs did.

At the wake, we sat on plastic chairs while the despairing family sobbed over the tiny body. "Why?" wailed the mother.

"Why?" my broken heart echoed.

When the time for the service came, Nate stood up and told one story. The story of the man Jesus who was called to come and heal a dear friend who was sick. He had been healing people for a while, so everyone knew he could do it.

But he didn't go.

He waited for several days, and his friend died, leaving two sisters bereft. Then, finally, too late, Jesus went. The sisters were sitting in devastation with their friends. When they saw Jesus, they both had the same question. "Why didn't you come? Why didn't you stop this?"

In answer, Jesus wept.

The story of Lazarus ends with Jesus opening the tomb, calling to his friend, and raising the dead back to life again. The answer to the question "why?" was given right then and there, as he showed his power in a new and life-changing way.

But that day twelve years ago, standing over the body of a beautiful little girl who should have still been alive, the end of Lazarus's story was not the comfort anyone needed. Nate did not offer promises that the child would find life again in heaven. He didn't talk about Jesus' power and his purpose in all things. Some things are not ours to promise or explain.

Jesus wept. That's where we lingered that day. He let his friend die when he could have prevented it. He let his other friends suffer the unimaginable loss of their brother. Why? Only he knows.

But it wasn't because he didn't care.

It tore his heart out to see their pain. And though he didn't stop it from coming, he did come and share it with them. He who made each person at that graveside, at every graveside, who loved them enough to die for them, felt their grief multiplied by his infinite capacity. He truly was a man of sorrow.

At the end of the story, I stood up in that dark and horrible place of loss and sang the simple words we would sing with the children when they came each week. Jesus loves me. This I know.

It's literally all I know.

29

Of Course I'm Going To Catch The Puke If I Can

My youngest child has always been a mystery to me. As I write this, I've known her for eleven years, and it's taken all this time to even sort of understand what makes her tick. When she was a baby, she was so content that she sometimes got lost in the chaos of her older siblings. Her own additions to the crazy were always...unexpected.

We moved home from Argentina right after Lucy turned two. The spring leading up to the move was one of the most stressful times of my life.[1] In the last weeks that we were in our tiny house, we moved all three kids into one bedroom to sleep at night. Ellie and Scott had bunk beds already, so it was just a matter of putting the pack-n-play into their room and then going in thirty-seven times each night to tell everyone to GOTOSLEEP.

---

[1] And since it culminated in packing up everything we owned and starting over in another country, it should probably win some sort of prize

We developed a routine. Lucy went down first, hopefully falling asleep like the easy little toddler she was, then the older children were tucked in, given one last warning about not waking their sister, and everyone settled in. We had a giant box fan to provide white noise and air circulation. It worked like a charm. Which is to say, everyone slept as much or as little as they had ever slept in any other sleeping arrangement we had ever tried.

One night near the end, this routine having played out pretty well, Nate and I settled in to watch some TV and try to shed some of the stress of the day. No sooner had we turned it on, though, than the power cut out. The TV. The lights. Our fan. The fan in the kids' room.

Yeah.

The white noise died. The baby was startled awake. She began to cry. The older kids helpfully yelled that the baby was crying.

I admit that normally when my expectation of a relaxing evening is thwarted by unsleeping children, I'm not the most gracious of mothers. But this was an act of God, so I tried to rise to the occasion. I ran to scoop up my sobbing toddler. Nate verified that the blackout was the whole neighborhood and not just our house, so we let the big kids join us on the couch for family snuggle time.

Ellie and Scott were thrilled. Something dramatic had happened. They were up late, and their dad would tell stories. I hoped they would be stories about sunny days and rainbows. Something that would entertain the older kids and maybe help Lucy forget that she was in the dark.

My sweet baby was not over the shock of her rude awakening. I held her close and whispered comforting words, but she only sobbed harder and harder. Then harder. I was learning the hard way that Lucy is not a fan of surprises. And she had more lessons for me. She sobbed so hard that night that she triggered her gag reflex and, just as I reassured her again that she was safe and loved, she threw up all over me.

"What's wrong?" Nate asked at my strangled cry of horror.

"She puked on me!"

"Mommy," said Ellie, "what's 'puked?'"

"Throw up! Puke is throw up!"

So there I was, in the middle of a massive life transition, sitting in the dark, covered in puke, holding a still-crying toddler while a six-year-old and a four-year-old danced around the shadows chanting "Lucy puked on Mommy! Lucy puked on Mommy!"

In case you're wondering, I did not see the humor in the situation and laugh it off. But I didn't sit there in despair either. In fact, writing this today, eight years later, I don't remember exactly how I felt in that moment. I didn't have the luxury of examining my feelings. What I remember is what I did. I gave my baby one more hug and kiss, and then I cleaned up all her vomit.

Do you know how hard it is to clean up vomit when there is no light?

Nate, God bless him, found candles and clean clothes. And he handled the older kids while I changed (though I seem to recall that his "handling" was mostly joining in their laughing chant). Eventually Lucy settled down, and the power came back, and at some point, everyone slept.

But no one in our family has ever forgotten that night.

I'm not sure why it was so legendary. It wasn't our only experience with blackouts or our only sleepless night. It wasn't my lowest emotional point, and it certainly wasn't the only time I've been puked on by my children.

Maybe it was the things we learned. Ellie and Scott learned the meaning of the word "puke." Nate learned where I kept the candles. I learned that my youngest is prone to emotional vomiting and that my older children will always be there for me in any crisis to crack jokes at my expense.[2]

Or maybe what really made it memorable was the darkness.

Nate and I are all about plans. We believe in doing things for a reason, and we have often had the privilege of being able to choose our future with a measure of control.

---

[2] Naturally, this makes me incredibly proud. Chips off old blocks, etc.

When we first talked about getting married, he told me about his plan to move to Argentina, and it felt like everything in my life came together to make sense. When things fell apart in our first church plant, we already had a plan for what was next to sustain us through that loss and failure.

On that night of power loss and puking, though, we knew the life we had planned wasn't going to happen, and we had no clear picture of what our new life was going to look like. We were thirty-five and about to start over again with three kids in tow. Talk about feeling your way through the dark.

It was everything I hated. It was pain with no sure and quick way to heal. It was questions with the most unsatisfying answers. It was the loss of so many bright things without knowing when the sun would come out again.

But that night the loss of light was not so very terrible. That night I found that in the dark we could still do what we had to do. In the dark we could still clean up each other's messes, we could still let each other know we weren't alone, we could still laugh and maybe even do a little dance.

In the dark we could still create a story that would be told over and over through the years.

And the story wouldn't ignore the dark. The story would be *about* the dark. And we would laugh about it just the same.

Afterword

If I were going to keep one of those old cross-stitched pillows from my childhood, it would be the one that says "The Joy Of The Lord Is My Strength." The words have been worn to death maybe, but they are unfailingly true. Probably because they're straight from Nehemiah, one of the Bible's many stories about battles against overwhelming odds.

Don't let anyone tell you that the joy of the Lord is some spiritual thing that has nothing to do with happiness. True, it's deeper than physical pleasure or momentary enjoyment, but joy means exactly what it sounds like it means. Being joyful is having a light heart. It's finding contentment with what is. It's laughing because you want to.

The miracle of laughter is that it can live right in the middle of pain. One minute I can't wrap my mind around the horror of my circumstances and the next, I am laughing, a brief reminder that I am still myself. No matter what has happened or will happen, the darkness doesn't define me.

This isn't an act of denial. It's a beautiful paradox. Joy can live alongside sorrow, and laughter can live alongside pain, and the two don't have to be at war. They can just be.

We can just be. In pain and full of joy all at the same time.

But please don't hear me saying that this joy is something you can muster up on your own. Laughing isn't another duty you have to add to your list of daily struggles (or failures). This joy I keep talking about? It's the joy *of the Lord*. It's his. Like all kids, we do nothing to earn our inheritance. We just hang around him, live in his house, ask him for what we need, complain, yell, smile, say thanks, learn from him even while sometimes actively trying not to. We get what belongs to our father just by being his children. His household is a place of joy in the midst of pain. We just have to make ourselves at home.

When Lucy was a few weeks old and we were still forming relationships in the new community where we lived, I was invited to visit a local soup kitchen to explore the possibility of partnering with them. Early one morning, I strapped my newborn to my chest, put a coat over both of us, and went to the tiny cement building that so many of my neighbors depended on for food. All day, as I peeled hard boiled eggs and washed dishes and talked with the woman who organized the place, I was reaching around the warmth of that little bundle.

"Welcome to your life, baby," I told her when she shifted her head. "This is what we do."

These days, when we're in church singing, sometimes ten-year-old Lucy will come up close and wrap her arms around me and rest her head on my chest, just where it rested all those years ago. I hug her and I sing, and I think about how much and how little has changed.

This is our life. This is what we do. It's a life of joy and also a life that's come at a cost. I'm intensely aware that more costs lie ahead.

It's harder to trust God with my children's future than with my own. I'd love for their happiness to be completely free from pain, but they are God's children as much as they are mine, and the world he made is not a tame one. It's equal parts wonderful and terrifying.

As I write these words, we are quarantined inside our house during the first world-wide pandemic in a hundred years. Last night, my daughter spiked a fever, and though I know she is young and strong and will almost certainly be fine, I am reminded again of how easily all that we have could be taken away.

As a mom, I understand the driving desire that caused mankind to build the tower of Babel. If I could keep all my loved ones in one place, as we are today, could make a mighty fortress that would keep us all safe, I would do it in an instant.

But God has a different plan. He is spinning us outward, spinning my children outward, to fill the earth and subdue it. They have places to go and worlds to conquer.

It will be pain and it will be joy. They will cry and they will laugh. And so will I.

And we'll fill the darkness with little sparks, accepting that some will quickly sputter out, accepting that only a few will kindle fires that last. But when our fires die, we will grieve them even as we light more, knowing that nothing lasts forever but where joy once was, it can come again.

And again.

And again.

Until the daylight we're waiting for finally dawns.

Special Thanks

Thank you to Nate, who trusted me with stories that are as much his as mine, and to Ellie, Scott, and Lucy, who graciously resigned themselves. In every way, this would have been impossible without you.

And thanks to Jessica, friend and editor extraordinaire, for getting me to finish line without falling on my face. You are always kinder than I deserve.

About the Author

Deborah Dunlevy is married to her best friend, Nate. Together they've made three weird and wonderful children, written nine books, failed to start two church communities, and helped start two that are miraculously still alive. She lives in Indianapolis where she writes novels and loves on an extended community of odd but resilient humans.

Deb loves stories of all kinds and would welcome hearing yours. You can write her at debdunlevy@madisonhousepublishing.com.

Other Books By Deborah Dunlevy

The Book of Sight

The Broken Circle

The Secret Source

The Poisoned Cure

The Shattered Heart

Una

Twin

Made in the USA
Monee, IL
19 April 2021